T0195079

Belongings

A LIFE OF COLLECTING AND TRAVELING

ZUZANA PLESA

authorHOUSE®

AuthorHouse™
1663 Liberty Drive
Bloomington, IN 47403
www.authorhouse.com
Phone: 833-262-8899

© 2022 Zuzana Plesa. All rights reserved.

No part of this book may be reproduced, stored in a retrieval system, or transmitted by any means without the written permission of the author.

Some of the names have been changed to protect individual privacy.

Published by AuthorHouse 01/06/2022

ISBN: 978-1-6655-4722-2 (sc)
ISBN: 978-1-6655-4721-5 (hc)
ISBN: 978-1-6655-4728-4 (e)

Library of Congress Control Number: 2021925053

Print information available on the last page.

Any people depicted in stock imagery provided by Getty Images are models, and such images are being used for illustrative purposes only. Certain stock imagery © Getty Images.

This book is printed on acid-free paper.

Because of the dynamic nature of the Internet, any web addresses or links contained in this book may have changed since publication and may no longer be valid. The views expressed in this work are solely those of the author and do not necessarily reflect the views of the publisher, and the publisher hereby disclaims any responsibility for them.

Scripture quotations marked NIV are taken from the Holy Bible, New International Version®. NIV®. Copyright © 1973, 1978, 1984 by International Bible Society. Used by permission of Zondervan. All rights reserved. [Biblica]

Contents

Dedication

To my parents
John Plesa and Anna Jozefek Plesa
And to my sister
Elizabeth Plesa Rhoads

Acknowledgements

To Suzanne Lieurance who kept me focused for a whole year resulting in a first draft.

To Amanda Morris who read my chapters and gave me valuable suggestions and insights.

To Joey Madia who read my entire manuscript and provided important feedback.

Special thanks to Kathrin Asper Jungian Analyst who helped me through the individuation process

To Jim Rector and Linda Smith who made me feel like family and supported me in my endeavors.

To Ralph Henson who patiently listened to several chapters.

To Ann Zloch Gouldsbury a life time friend who kept me intellectually aware with articles, emails and books.

To Bernice Hornak Sand who is a master of the art of listening and has been a life long friend.

I thank God for giving me the ability and strength to write this memoir.

To Kevin Haas for all his technical support.

To Grace Scofield for typing my manuscript.

Chapter 1

The Wrong Medicine

It is a sunny June morning in Wurzburg, Germany, 1979. I take my usual walk through the vineyards with my German friend Inga. Grapes are beginning to ripen. We discuss the tasty wine we know they will make. Energized by our walk, I go back to my apartment and prepare to go to work at the high school on Leighton Barracks Army Post. It is exam week at Wurzburg American High in Germany, and my English classes will be taking their final exams. The drive to school is short, but along the way I admire the red geraniums in the boxes. Every house has them.

Ten minutes later, I arrive at school, park my car and walk up to my second-floor classroom, which is spacious with big windows. Sometimes the students would prefer to look out the window and observe the birds and trees instead of concentrating on their lesson. I too at times am distracted. Soon the students will arrive, so I sit at my desk and plan out the time when I will grade the exams and turn in my grades. There is so much to do at the end of a school year, and I look forward to relaxing during summer vacation. I will travel to New York City and enjoy the plays on Broadway. The first bell rings, sounding like the booming gong opening the Stock Market. I have to stop dreaming because the students are starting to enter. This is their last day with me.

As they take their seats, I greet the students by name, noticing that a few of them barely have their eyes open and look as if they just rolled out of bed, while others seem eager to begin summer vacation by the water. They ask me if they can leave right after they finish the exam. There are a few sad faces because they will miss their friends. One student asks to go to the bathroom, another needs a drink of water to take his medication and a third trips over his untied tennis shoe but is able to break his fall.

The second bell rings and the students quietly await distribution of the exam. I walk around the classroom to make sure everyone is on task. One student needs another pen because his ran out of ink, so I give him one of the spares I keep in my desk. I observe the students while they are taking the exam. Some look anxious. Others breeze through and still others are rushing with one foot already in summer vacation. I observe their happy, sad and troubled faces, each of them unique.

Suddenly the assistant principal appears in the doorway and beckons for me to come outside. She has a serious look on her face, so I anticipate a problem. Is some parent upset with me? Is she going to fire me? My stomach starts to churn. She remains silent, handing me a paper with a Red Cross message. It reads, "Father fell down the stairs and died." I take a deep breath and hold back the tears. I place my hand on the wall to keep from passing out. The assistant principal quietly says, "I'm sorry for your loss. What can I do to help?"

Stumbling over my words, I manage to mumble, "I need to go home to New York City to help my mother and attend the funeral."

"I'll make plane reservations for you to fly to New York," she says.

"Thanks, I'll come see you after class."

I reenter the classroom. Although I feel like a squeezed lemon whose juice is gone, I have a class exam to monitor. Memories of my father flood my mind. I think of the time I had spent with him at his candy store. I could have all the ice cream, candy, soda and malted milk

I wanted. I loved helping make the malted milk and drinking it as if it were my final drink on earth. When there were no customers, we had fun arranging the soda bottles according to flavor. Grape soda was my favorite, so I put those bottles in front of the others.

The candy store was my world of fun and imagination. When the store was closed, we would visit St. Mary's Park, and my father would put me on the swings. I felt like I was flying and would imagine being in a beautiful castle surrounded by water whose waves would draw me like the drinking of a malted milk through a straw. I loved going down the slide in the park because I felt carefree, as though I could conquer the world.

As I watch my students concentrate on their exam, I realize that no one is going to tell me jokes and make me laugh on such a regular basis. I will not be able to eat his pork chops, peach cake and mushroom soup three of my favorites. All I have left are memories of my father. I believe he was the only one who ever loved me. I feel all alone and wonder how I will go on. All the once green trees now look black and dark. Even the sky, still blue, looks both bleak and threatening. Class is almost over. I bring myself back to reality and prepare to dismiss my students. I collect the exam papers and wish the students a pleasant summer. They wave goodbye as they depart.

I am already gone from their minds. After class, I go to the restroom and cry and cry until I have no more tears. My father, who had always been there for me, is gone. I cannot think straight and do not know what to do. I dry my eyes and go to the office of the assistant principal. She has already made arrangements for me to fly to New York City for the funeral. She has also made reservations for me to return to Germany in ten days because I have a graduate class to complete and preliminary exams to take for the doctoral program I have started.

I thank her for her support, before driving home to my cold, damp apartment. It seems even drearier now. I call my mother to tell her I am coming home. She answers the phone and says, "Where are you"? I have to remind her that I am still in Germany and only just received the message of my father's death.

"When will you be home?"

"Soon," I whisper.

"Oh… okay," she sighs.

All the arrangements for the viewing, funeral and burial are made. The funeral will be on my mother's 62nd birthday. What a sad birthday it will be. She cries while she tells me of my father's accidental death. He fell down the stairs at home. I let out a scream and utter, "Oh my God … no," reminding me of Jesus on the cross when he cried out.

I hope the German landlady isn't home to hear me. I can't even say my last goodbye to my father. The accidental death has robbed me of my farewell. My mother's efficiency seems to have disappeared, replaced with confusion. I say, "I'll see you soon," Now I am even more anxious to get home and support my mother. I still have to grade my exams and turn in the grades the next day. I start on the schoolwork, even though my mind is on my mother and the death of my father. I cry while grading the papers, making sure the tears do not fall on the students' papers.

After I am done, I have to pack my suitcase, including a black dress and black scarf because we are a traditional family and black is worn to funerals. After packing, I need some fresh air, so I walk in the vineyards to relieve my anxiety. The vineyards do not look as bright and inviting as they did during my morning walk.

My mind once again wanders to the times, my father took me to St. Mary's Park where I would climb the steep rocks and enjoy the view of colorful flowers at the bottom. I then remember the flower garden with red roses that my father planted and maintained. He had a green thumb. The fragrance of his lilac tree comes back to me as I walk. When

I return to the apartment, I think about our house in New York and how different it will be without him.

Who will maintain the garden and make the repairs? My mother is not handy, so how will she survive in the house? I have many questions and no answers. Having no appetite, I do not eat. I just drink water. I try to go to bed, but I have a hard time sleeping. I pray and read my Bible for most of the night. Prayer brings me comfort.

The next morning, I bring my grades to school, and then I am ready to go to the airport. The assistant principal agrees to drive me to Frankfurt. I am grateful. She insists that I complete my course for the doctoral program I have started and take my exams. I don't want to think about the course, so I go along with what she suggests. I leave her at the airport entrance and wait to board the plane. Once on the plane, I cry, trying to write a farewell letter to my father. How will I start? I decide to address the letter as Dear Tata because *Tata* is Slovak for father and I always addressed him in that way. As the tears flow, the memories come quickly, and I try to write them down so I will not forget them. The soldier sitting next to me asks if I am okay. I say, "I am going to my father's funeral." He expressed his sympathy. I thought I would be going home on vacation but today my mission was my letter:

Dear Tata,

A smile, a joke, a comforting word for a child in pain. Somehow you understood when no one else would. I wish I could have helped to relieve your pain, but I felt helpless in my finiteness. I have not left words unsaid because our avenues of communication were open the words"" I love you" were spoken in life. The ability to care and at times to sense the unspoken were gifts you shared with me. Your life perhaps was misunderstood by many but there is one who saw the aspects of untapped potential the quiet sensitivity. You didn't make TIME magazine, but you passed on to a daughter many humble traits. You taught me to catch a fish, to tie a shoe, to see the humor in life, to hum a tune and to see the beauty in each human life no matter what the color of the skin. Even though ill yourself, you gave of yourself to an old Black man lying next to you in a hospital bed. The scene touched me deeply.

I regret that you won't be here when I am called Dr. Zuzana Plesa for, I have only begun that pursuit. But I trust you will know about it. The tears I shed are tears of my loss and emptiness, for death always leaves a void. The greatest gift you gave me was to introduce me to the Lord Jesus Christ and to trust Him always. What more can a child ask of a parent! Now that you are with the Lord, I patiently wait and trust God's timing that we will meet again at Jesus' feet. For we know that this life is only a beginning and not a termination. I bid you farewell until we meet again.

Lovingly,
Your daughter,
Zuzana

It took me the eight hours on the plane to write this letter to my father. I felt great comfort and relief after I had written it. It is as if the paper and pen absorbed some of my grief and I felt a calmness and peace overtake me for a while. I placed it in my carry on so I could read it at the funeral. The taxi driver asked why I was so sad, and I told him what had happened. He was sympathetic and tried to express comforting words, but I just wanted him to be quiet. I was relieved when we arrived at our house. My mother was on the front porch awaiting my arrival. She hugged me and held on to me tightly. She said, "I am so glad that you are finally here."

We went inside the house and she showed me where my father had fallen and hit his head. There was a dent in the wall where his head had struck it. I could hardly bear to look, but I did, I wanted to kick the wall that caused the accident. After that I could not eat so I sat down at the table with a glass of water and talked with my mother. I tried to understand her grief. We had to take care of business, so she said we would have two days of viewing and then the funeral would be on the third day. The next two days would be spent at the funeral parlor, which was located in Manhattan.

A neighbor volunteered to drive us there so we would not have to take the subway. We had no car of our own. We were grateful for the offer. My sister, who was pregnant, arrived from California on the first day of the viewing. She came straight to the funeral parlor. I was happy to see her. We could share memories of my father. At the viewing the fragrance of the flowers was overwhelming. Flowers from relatives, friends and even from my high school faculty surrounded the coffin. It was as if my father was in his garden. My sister, mother and I knelt at the coffin to say our goodbyes. We were dressed in black. My aunt Kristine dressed in black and my father's youngest sister came and offered her sympathy. She gave me a picture of my grandmother holding my father on her lap when he was about six months old. I had the picture framed and treasured it. Aunt Kristine said, "Your father was always curious and creative in life. As a young boy he would make brooms of straw and sell them for pocket money."

Hearing stories about my father's life comforted me. My uncle Paul came, my father's older and only brother and said he would miss his brother. He said, "Your father had a keen knowledge of the stock market, and I would often call him for tips on what to buy." Yes, my father was a businessman at heart. Seeing family and friends supported me. The need for community became very clear for me and something I missed living in Germany. The pastor of Holy Trinity Lutheran Church came to the viewing and offered prayers. Then I read the letter that I had written to my father while flying home. My mother was concerned that I would not be able to read it without an emotional breakdown. I knew I could do it. My father had taught me to be resilient, and I soldiered on. Touched by my letter, people complimented and thanked me. The pastor asked for a copy to be printed in the church bulletin so others could read it. I gladly agreed. After two days of viewing, we prepared for the funeral service.

June 15, 1979, my sister and I wished my mother a happy 62nd birthday. Then we had to prepare for my father's funeral. All three of us, still dressed in black, were driven to the church by a friend. Upon arrival at the church, we were escorted to the front pew. Several family members were already there. With all the flowers and organ music playing, the church made me think that it would be like Heaven. Once the casket was rolled to the front, my body froze. My mother and sister looked stiff as boards. I hoped that the service would go quickly because I was already hot, restless and anxious. I wondered how Jackie Kennedy was able to go through the funeral of her husband, the assassinated president.

The service did go quickly, and I think my father would have appreciated it. He did not like things to be drawn out. At the end we thanked the people for coming and went to the waiting limousine to take us to the cemetery in Brooklyn about 45 minutes away. Once at the cemetery, we all gathered at the family burial plot and watched the casket being lowered into the ground. We put roses from my father's garden on his casket our final good bye to him.

His life on this earth was finished at the age of 71. I felt like a part of me had been buried with him. The limousine drove us to a Czech restaurant named Praha in Manhattan to participate in the funeral dinner with family and friends to celebrate my father's life. My mother said he would have wanted us to celebrate with a good meal. There were fifty people in attendance including family and friends. Our pastor sat at the head table with my mother, aunts and uncles. My sister and I sat with our cousins from my father's side. That was the best part of it because we exchanged stories about our lives. Two of my cousins were teachers, so we could talk about our students. My sister and other cousins were stay at home moms, so they talked about their children. The food choices were pork, chicken and beef. I chose chicken because it is the safest choice. It was delicious. The presence of family and friends helped lessen the grief for the moment.

One of our friends drove us home. The house seemed different without my father. We had eaten at the restaurant, so we did not have to worry about cooking. My sister and I sorted my father's clothes. We remembered the pants he wore when he took us to the park. The long white apron he wore in the candy store was there. We packed all the clothes and the following day we brought them to Goodwill. We talked about playing in St. Mary's Park and what fun we had. We tried to clean the house for my mother because she was confused about everything.

A few days later, after my sister left, my mother was even sadder, but I was still there for a few more days. I made meals for us, did the laundry and cleaned the house. When I told my mother that I had to return to Germany to take exams she fell apart. She cried like a frightened child soon to be abandoned. I then made the decision to return to New York after the exams and spend the summer with my mother. I was concerned because she did not seem to be functioning well. I asked my neighbor to check on her until I returned. I flew back to Germany. Once back in my apartment, I tried to study for exams, but my mind was on my mother. Although I was in no shape to take the exams, I went through with it. I hardly read the questions and randomly selected answers. I should have postponed them. I just had to finish and return to help my mother. Several days later I was informed that I had failed the exams. I of course was not surprised. I was apathetic and listless. I was given the opportunity to take additional courses in the fall and then retake the exam. I declined. I was done for the moment. I had disappointed myself and my father. I had not listened to my own feelings about waiting but instead plunged ahead in a reckless way, setting myself up for failure.

I promised myself and my father that someday I would complete my doctorate, but not now. I didn't learn to think before I leapt.

I spent the summer in New York City and helped my mother take care of the house. She signed up with a senior citizens group and attended their lunches each day of the week. The bus picked her up and brought her home. With the senior group and my neighbor's visits, my mother seemed to function a little better. I did see a few Broadway plays and visited museums. My mother and I visited the cemetery named Linden Hill, which is where we have our family plot. We planted a few red geraniums that we had dug up from my father's garden. He would have his geraniums to comfort him.

By his grave, my mother said, "I feel good about creating beauty around his grave. It continues to connect me to him."

I quietly agreed as I continued planting. We didn't do much talking, instead just doing the work of planting the five geraniums. It felt good to get our hands soiled and to feel the earth. My father would have appreciated our efforts to surround him with flowers.

I returned to Germany at the end of the summer a changed person. The sparkle in my green eyes disappeared and my smile rarely appeared. I had a ghost like appearance. I lost a lot of weight within a short period of time because I had no appetite. Not only did I lose my father, I failed in the doctoral program.

I did not know where I belonged. I believed in God, but I seemed to need a physical father for comfort. To alleviate the depression that filled me, I started to shop. I would make weekly trips to the pottery factory and collect red plates, cups and saucers. I had a twelve-piece setting.

I bought crystal vases and glasses that would fill an entire crystal factory. Each purchase would give me a temporary high. I bought white Rosenthal china because the rose pattern reminded me of my father's garden. I bought dolls and named them after my mother, sister and aunts. I could not stop shopping. I did not give thought to where I would put the purchases or what I would do with them. My apartment became so cluttered that it became difficult to clean. The German landlady told me I had to get rid of some things. I resented her because she invaded my privacy. I paid rent but she thought she could come in whenever she liked and check up on my housekeeping skills.

She said, "You must clean regularly, and you must wash your windows every week" to which I replied, "Housekeeping is my business and not yours."

Although I hated to move, but I did to a bigger apartment that gave me a little more room to buy things. I promised myself that, when I returned to the States, I would never live in another rented place where a landlord told me how to live. I wanted my own house. To reach that goal I would have to start saving money instead of buying things. Having my own house would be very freeing, and I now had a reason to stop buying and start saving.

Or perhaps I would continue to buy things to fill up my house.

Trying to save money for a house did slow down my buying. My father had taught me to save my money and to buy everything with cash. I could apply that learning to my life. Memories of my father and experiences with him kept cropping up. Our trip to Slovakia is one that will stay with me forever.

Chapter 2

My First Visit to Vrbovce, Slovakia

Before I started attending Fuller Seminary in August 1973, my father and I took a trip to Slovakia that July. He wanted me to see where he grew up. My father was born in Lansford, Pennsylvania, but his parents, who were immigrants from Czechoslovakia, took him back to Chvojnica at an early age. He returned to America at the age of 18. He had acquired some cooking skills in Vienna and put them to work as a chef in New York City. It has been forty years since he has seen Czechoslovakia, although I had grown up hearing stories about Slovakia. I dreamed of the village of Vrbovce, and the sections of Chvojnica and Stephanova all my life. Since the only means of transportation was by foot, my father had to walk miles to go to the center of town for shoes or medications. The road to town was hilly and long. I felt a thrill inside me knowing that I was walking on the same road my father and grandfather once did. My father made brooms of straw and carried them to town to sell.

All he ate on the way was a slice of dried bread. He drank from a jug of water. Now I better understood why my father appreciated public transportation in New York City.

We ate well in New York City, and I am grateful that it was more than dried bread and water. We even had an abundance of milk.

Now, in July, of 1973, at the age of thirty-one, he wanted me to see our ancestral land. My father's sister, Betty, still lived in Slovakia and expected our visit. But when we arrived at the airport in Bratislava, there was no one to meet us. My father found a couple willing to drive us the 250 kilometers to Chvojnica for $70 American dollars. After we arrived, my aunt explained the mix-up; when my father wrote to say we were coming, he forgot to include the date and time. My father was not a letter writer and I should have known better than to depend on him to make the arrangements with my Aunt Betty. He was already drinking excessively, and he barely wrote a readable letter.

I was disappointed in his inability to complete the simple letter task. It made me sad to realize that I could no longer depend on him to even do this. My aunt would monitor his drinking throughout the trip, and I was grateful for her assistance.

For now, we piled into the small Slovak car and started on our way. The neglected roads, unpainted buildings and broken windows were signs of Communist control. The remote, rural people and their villages were a last priority because they were so far away from Mother Russia.

The village of Vrbovce is situated in the Little White Carpathian Mountains, at the foot of Zalostina hill, which is supposed to signify winter and death. To the south is Vesny Hill, where spring and new life originate. A mosaic of meadows, pastures and fields, beech and oak woods surround Vrbovce. The brown soil and hilly country are ideal for potato growing and livestock production. The village is nestled in a valley and from each hill one could glimpse the red tile roofs along with the highest structure in town, the white church steeple. The Lutheran Church with its onion dome overlooks Vrbovce as the eye of God. The green trees interspersed among the homes interlock as the pieces of a puzzle. I feel proud to come from such a picturesque area of the world.

Zalostina has its own story. While a mother was cooking dinner, she asked her daughter to bring some water. The daughter ran off to the well. The mother waited, becoming impatient and angry. She shouted,

"Turn into stone where you are standing." Her daughter did turn to stone and did not return. When the mother saw the stone stature, she started to weep, "Oh I am a poor mother, what have I done to my daughter?" The hill gets its name from this story. Zalostny literally means poor or sad in Slovak. I enjoyed hearing stories like these. It is hard to believe that God has given such beautiful trees and hills to my ancestors. They must have felt closer to their maker on the mountain top.

The hills of Vrbovce were beautiful, and they were alive with the sound of music, like in the movie of that name. They seemed to beckon me to thank God for the beauty around me. Red Spanish tile roofs were all around me in the village center. My father frequently talked about the durability of these roofs. As I observed them from the hills, they appeared like dancing figures in red outfits.

Vrbovce means "Avenue of the Willows," and I understood why the willow has always been the favorite family tree. It was our tree of life. My grandfather Paul Plesa would be the trunk of the willow tree and my father and I the branches. The roots of the willow tree are remarkable for their toughness, size and tenacity to live. I have the qualities of the willow tree. Knowing my roots gives me a sense of security and rootedness. The area is surrounded by several settlements and the section of Vrbovce named Stefanova on the northwest was where my mother's ancestors settled. My mother was born in Muskegon Heights, Michigan but was brought up in Stefanova. She returned to America when she was fourteen. Stephanova had a fairy tale view of the village of Vrbovce and would be considered choice property. Chvojnica, the village of my father's family, borders Vrbovce on the west. I felt I had come to the promised land. It would be difficult for me to leave such a beautiful area and settle in New York City. The visit helped me to imagine the fear and loneliness my father felt leaving Vrbovce and arriving in New York City. He arrived at night by boat and thought the big buildings were mountains. He was excited to come to a mountainous city but disappointed when he realized that they were skyscrapers.

After 40 years, my father could still direct the driver to my aunt Betty's house in Chvojnica. Hate was the section of Chvojnica where my Aunt Betty lived. Betty was dressed in her royal blue Kroj, (costume) when she came out to meet us. She was speechless for a few moments, and then her tears started to flow. She and my father resembled each other. Their oval shaped faces and slight body build were similar. My aunt's maiden name was Plesa and she married a man, not related to her, also named Plesa. This is a common name in Chvojnica, just as Smith is common in America. To distinguish one Plesa from another the families were given additional names related to their occupation. My grandfather was a blacksmith, so we were Plesa-Kovac.

I then met my uncle Paul Plesa for the first time and then met my cousin Paul. This was my family and I experienced joy in meeting them. Uncle Paul was a storyteller and kept us laughing with his jokes. Their farmhouse was simple but neat. It was a real farmhouse with no indoor toilet. I had to go through the barn and shoo the chickens away to reach the outhouse. An outside pump which I quickly learned to operate furnished household water. I was not accustomed to such a primitive life. I was glad to connect with my roots, but I felt like I belonged in America and was grateful that they immigrated. I liked the convenience of an indoor toilet.

That evening, we sat down to a dinner table of bread, homemade Kolbasa, potatoes and tomatoes. Slivovica (plum brandy) flowed in abundance and made everyone happy except me.

I am uncomfortable around people who drink because I saw the changes in my father. I vowed never to drink alcohol because of my fear of becoming addicted to it. Coffee, tea and milk were also available, which is much more to my taste. The family told me that I was not a true Slovak because I drink only non-alcoholic beverages. This made me feel like I didn't belong, but I stuck to my truth that I would not drink alcohol.

The following day we met the rest of the Plesa clan: cousin, John, and his wife Mary, and their children, Libusha, Vera and John. Libusha became my friend for three weeks and we saw Vrbovce together. She was twenty years old, and short and slender. We wore the same size clothing, so I gave her a few of my dresses. My father took me to the house where he grew up, a simple cottage with a stream running in front of it. He had tears in his eyes because he had fond memories of growing up in that house with his parents and siblings. The current owners allowed us to look around. What an experience to walk on the same wood floors that my ancestors had trod. I saw the barn my great grandfather Martin Plesa had built in 1872. We climbed the ladder and read his name along with that of my great grandmother, Betty Zloch. It was the most beautiful barn I have ever seen. It is made of birch wood and can hold many bales of hay. The roof is made of red Spanish tile that can be seen at a distance. Twenty cows can make their home in the barn. The barn became for me a symbol of the artist in my great grandfather.

The present owner said to me, "You cannot forget about that barn." I don't. Whenever I return to Vrbovce, I always visit the barn.

On Sunday we attended services at the Lutheran Church in Vrbovce, the major church in the village. Most of the people there are Lutheran. The men sit on one side and the women on the other. My cousins all wear the Kroj, which is a white pleated skirt, a blue vest and apron. The white blouse with puffy sleeves has blue ribbons and lace on the sleeves. The lace headdress covers the entire head, so no hair is visible. The Kroj gives my cousins a royal look. I stand out in my white and blue flowered American dress. The next week I am dressed in a green and orange Kroj, those colors signifying that I am single, and I am told I look like a real "Slovak woman." Outwardly, in a Kroj, I am a Slovak but not when I don't drink alcohol. That puzzles me. At times I belong and at other times I do not. I felt closer to God being in the church of my ancestors. Being in church and knowing that my grandfather was a believer, makes me feel even better about attending Seminary. I think my grandparents would have been proud that I was a woman of faith.

During that first visit, I learned that there were many Jewish families in Vrbovce until World War II. The synagogue was gone, and the Jewish cemetery was overgrown. Some of the town elders told me that the names of Jozefek, Melicharek and Stefek are the names of Jewish families. My mother was a Jozefek, her mother a Melicharek and my father's mother a Stefek. My parents were brought up as Slovak Lutherans and never mentioned anything about a Jewish background, but I believe we have one.

After church, we drove to Stephanova, met my mother's side of the family and saw the house where she grew up. Aunt Kristine, my mother's youngest sister, greeted us at the door. My father and I knew Aunt Kristine because she had visited us in America, but now, I also got to meet Uncle John and their children, Anna, Zuzana, Betty and John. I had heard about my cousins but meeting them for the first time was exciting. They were all married and lived in different parts of Vrbovce. Anna and Zuzana the two closest to me in age were married and lived in Vrbovce proper. Betty and John were nine years younger than me. All four cousins and their families attended a pig roast at Zuzana's house. We sang, danced to accordion music played by my cousin John ate pork and potatoes. After I met my cousins, I saw Deda, (grandfather) Jozefek, sitting in the kitchen with his cane. I ran over, and hugged him, shouting, "I am so happy to see you again!" I was excited to see him because he lived with us for nineteen years in New York but decided to return to Slovakia for his final years. My sister and I cried when he left America. He looked at me with his big blue eyes and white hair and said, "How pretty you look!" He showed me a map of Slovakia and described some of the surrounding villages. I am a geography teacher, so my interest in Slovak geography was peaked. He gave me the map as a gift. When he lived with us in New York, he would give me a dollar every Saturday, and I would tell everyone, "I am going to be rich!". My grandfather read the newspaper each day and would tell me about the stories he read. He was a good teacher. Both my father and grandfather made me feel special. Though I did not know it, this would be the last time I saw him, because he died just two months after I returned home.

Although I connected with my Slovak relatives because I speak Slovak, I still felt glad that my grandparents had immigrated to America and I was an American.

There were more educational and professional opportunities for me in America. I could not have survived as a farm laborer or a cook as most of my relatives did. I felt blessed to be an American and was grateful to my grandparents for taking the risk of leaving the homeland. I'm still longing to belong in America. Maybe I belong someplace else. I had the fantasy of living in Colorado because the mountains always looked inviting and drew me to them.

Chapter 3

Survival in Denver

"Why, my soul, are you downcast? Why so disturbed within me? Put you hope in God, for I will yet praise him, my Savior and my God." (Psalm 43:5)

Life was a roller coaster. My whole body felt heavy and depression controlled me for many days. Any slight failure on my part would make me fall to pieces. My family problems felt insurmountable. Teaching was just a job to earn some bread. After I moved to Denver in 1963, my relationship with God strengthened. I started to attend Good Shepherd Lutheran Church and the minister, Pastor Mendenhall, was really a man of faith.

"When I said, "My foot is slipping' "your unfailing love, Lord, supported me. When anxiety was great within me, your consolation brought me joy." (Psalm 94:18-19)

Pastor Mendenhall's sermons seemed to inspire me and keep me going, but I still suffered from anxiety and depression. I lacked the skills and inner strength to adjust to a new place. As a result, my inner turmoil increased. I felt like I did not belong any place on this earth. I kept blaming outer circumstances for my problems instead of looking inward. I did not know how to reach out to new people. Pastor Mendenhall even suggested I join another church where there were more professional and single people. His advice fell on deaf ears.

I seem to reject sound suggestions.

"Call to me and I will answer you and tell you great and unsearchable things you do not know." (Jeremiah 33:3)

"At times it was hard to believe that God really heard me, but I learned that His plan and timing do not always parallel mine. It takes faith to develop the patience to trust God. Joyce Meyer, a woman preacher, says "Go to the throne, instead of the phone." Her statement along with scripture have helped me through difficult times.

"I seek you with all my heart; do not let me stray from your commands." (Psalm 119:10)

"How did I manage to obtain a job in Denver? I had a connection through my father. I had obtained a summer job in the firm where my father worked. I was a listing clerk and would list the stocks and bonds that the company bought and sold. The Denver Public Schools had an account with Discount Corp of New York. The officer in charge of the Denver Public Schools account put me in contact with their treasurer. What a stroke of luck because I later learned that it was difficult for outsiders to secure a job in Denver. I flew to Denver for an interview and a few days later received a phone call that I had been hired. I was so excited to be moving to Denver for my first teaching job.

"The Lord will guide you always, he will satisfy your needs in a sun-scorched land and will strengthen your frame. You will be like a well-watered garden; like a spring whose waters never fail." (Isaiah 58:11)

My fantasy of living in Denver surrounded by the Rocky Mountains soon turned to a reality that I had not envisioned. My first teaching job was in a junior high school with five classes of social studies and one guidance group. I could handle the social studies, but I had no experience in psychology or counscling. How was I, at the age of 21 to handle these students with so many problems with abuse and family financial issues? I prayed daily for the strength to help my students when I myself felt very alone and vulnerable.

"No temptation has overtaken you except what is common to mankind. And God is faithful; he will not let you be tempted beyond what you can bear. But when you are tempted, he will also provide a way out so that you can endure it." (1 Corinthians 10:13)

Each day I felt that God gave me the strength to face the students and be supportive. I would listen to their stories of physical and sexual abuse because the students needed a listener without judgement. I would connect the students with those who could intervene and assist them. I started to realize that perhaps just listening was the gift I could give them. The school was large, so we had double sessions. I was assigned to the afternoon session from 12 to 5:30 p.m. I am a morning person, so the afternoon session was hard on me. I struggled to stay alert in the late afternoon. I wasn't as energetic with my late afternoon class as I was earlier in the day. By the grace of God, I learned to adjust my sleep and waking hours so I could better function at that time. I slept later into the morning so I would have enough rest to get through the day. Being rested made me a better teacher.

"Trust in the Lord with all your heart and do not lean on your own understanding. In all your ways acknowledge Him, and He will make your paths straight." (Proverbs 3:5-6)

A new job, city and apartment were almost too much stress at one time, but I believe that God's angels were watching over me and guided me through this difficult time. Going to church each Sunday gave me the community I needed for support. Prayer and journaling became my survival tools during my three years in Denver. I started to feel like I belonged, but my roommate left to take a job in Germany. I too decided to move and, not knowing where to go, I moved back to New York still looking to belong. Whenever things get uncomfortable or someone leaves, I want to move on too. I turned to the outer world for support instead of depending on God. I was not trusting God enough to remain in Denver.

Back in New York, I wondered why I returned. The family tension was still there, and I had no job, so I decided to pursue a master's degree at Hoftstra University. That would give me a constructive goal. I also applied for substitute teaching in the Bronx to earn some money to survive. I completed the Master's Degree in Education in one year. I had to find a job, so I took a job as an English teacher in a junior high school in the Bronx. The students were far more difficult than the ones I taught in Denver. I was living at home, trying to make peace with my parents and feeling that I did not belong. In addition, the teaching job was so very difficult. I did have supportive colleagues at the school and that helped me survive, but I knew I could not live this way for very long. I had to move. Where would I go? Where would I belong? I had heard about overseas schools that were part of the Department of Defense Dependents Schools from my roommate in Denver. I could travel to exciting places and have a job. The overseas schools provided transportation to a location, housing and shipment of a car and household goods. What a deal! If I stayed long enough, I would be eligible for a civil service pension. So, after being back in New York City for three years, I decided to apply for an overseas teaching job. I receive a job offer and I accept it with joy. A new place and a new start to feel like I belong.

Japan at Last… But First Guantanamo Bay, Cuba

My first assignment with the Department of Defense Dependents Schools was at Guantanamo Bay, Cuba. It was there that I saw wooden bowls and woven baskets in the exchange, and I start to buy things I didn't know existed. The excessive buying and accumulating of objects had started. Guantanamo was a small area, and we were not permitted to enter mainland Cuba. I started collecting things to entertain myself.

Wooden bowls and plates from Haiti, straw hats and baskets from Jamaica all were stuffed into my one room in Guantanamo.

Then, in May 1970, I hear about my next assignment, which was at Misawa Air Base in, Japan. This seemed like a dream come true. I already anticipate all the great shopping that would be available. So many nice things are made in Japan. Japan is an introverted country and as an introvert, I knew that I would fit in. The Japanese honor and respect nature, so maybe enjoying nature would help me decrease my collecting and buying.

Misawa is located on the main Japanese island of Honshu, on the southern shore of picturesque Lake Ogawara. The lake had been used by the Imperial Japanese Navy to practice for the attack on Pearl Harbor. The city of Misawa, which has a population of 43,000, is small and quaint with late-blooming flowers and changing colors of the trees.

The small-town atmosphere of Misawa made me long for a big city. Winters were long and spring brought in the thick sea fog. In summer, there was a rainy season. Misawa became a shopper's paradise for me. I made weekly trips to the dressmaker and had clothes made from silk, wool and cotton. The Japanese dressmaker put several patterns together and came up with a unique creation. I had a red cashmere coat with black fur trim made, which kept me nice and warm. Beautiful kimonos were reasonably priced, so I bought one in each color available.

Once I was settled in an apartment on base, I wrote to my high school pen-pal, Tetsuya who was in Tokyo, and said I would like to meet him. I wondered what he would look like and how we would relate to each other. I felt a bit nervous. I hoped he could show me all the good shopping places in Tokyo.

Over Labor Day weekend, I got three days off, so I decided to travel to Tokyo. Since this was an overnight train trip, I invited a colleague named Carolyn to go along. We boarded the train on Friday evening, and not having thought ahead to reserve a berth, we spent an uncomfortable night sitting up. The train was crowded, and smelled of fish.

We planned to stay with Joyce, a mutual friend stationed at Tachikowa Air Base. The subway system was confusing, though, and we took the wrong train. After several mix-ups, we finally arrive at the Tachikowa Station and took a cab to Joyce's quarters.

The three of us went to the Officer's Club for breakfast and dined on eggs, waffles, fruit and cheese. What a treat! This was far superior to the normal Japanese breakfast of fish soup and raw eggs. Afterward we went to the Base Exchange, which was three times bigger than the BX at Misawa. It seemed as large as a shopping mall, and it contained everything one might need furniture, books, clothing all in one building. I thought at the time that buying things would help me belong, so my eyes bulged with delight at the sight of Japanese dolls, silk scarves and pottery. I had to restrain myself or my first paycheck would be spent before earned.

Buying new and different things gave me a temporary elated feeling as nothing else could.

We finish out our on base shopping and left our purchases at Joyce's apartment. The three of us took off on the subway to find my pen pal and more shopping areas. According to his address, Tetsuya lived on the outskirts of Tokyo. Once again, we soon found that we had chosen the wrong direction. In halting English, the lady in a tourist office explained the problem and we were lucky enough to find a schoolboy who could speak English. He suggested we stop at a police station for directions and failing that try at a grocery store. No one we asked could speak English. While the boy did his best to translate, our only clue was the street name Izumi-so and the number of my pen pal's apartment. With the schoolboy and policeman accompanying us, we trudged around the busy neighborhood. People stare at us the out-of-place Americans. Three hours went by before we found the correct apartment house. The apartment building was three stories tall and painted a solid medium blue. There were no elevators in the building and climbing the stairs seemed like hiking up Mount Fuji. When we reached his floor, we knocked on the door. An attractive petite woman opened it. When she saw the policeman standing there, she looked puzzled and frightened. I showed her an old letter from Tetsuya and the light dawned. "Dozo," she exclaimed, which means, "Please come in." She was dressed in a blue kimono and cherry blossoms decorated her shiny black hair. Although she could not speak English, she said her name was Motoko and her husband was at work. The boy and policeman departed, leaving the three of us to fend for ourselves.

Somehow, I explained that Tetsuya was expecting my visit; that I had written a letter to him. Motoko offered green tea to everyone and introduced her two sons, five and seven years old. The living room of the apartment had a table in the center with a warmer beneath it. The walls were decorated with pictures of beautiful mountains and waterfalls. We sat on pillows on the floor. Two end tables housed white Japanese lamps with a cherry blossom pattern on them. A free-standing silk screen decorated with mandarin oranges stood in the far corner of the room.

After a while, when it was clear Tetsuya would not be home for a long time, I gave his wife my local telephone number. After many polite bows, we set off for the subway station. I wanted to hail a taxi but didn't know how. Once again, we struggled with the subway lines and made it safely back to Joyce's apartment. Tetsuya called later that evening full of apologies. He said he never received my letter and made arrangements to meet the next morning at 9:00 a.m. at Tachikowa Station. Having had enough of wandering around Tokyo, Joyce decided not to go along.

As it turned out, Tetsuya spoke flawless English and had a winning smile. He was much taller than most Japanese men and was dressed in a dark business suit. He hired a taxi to take us around the city to see the points of interest, including the Imperial Palace and a Shinto shrine. We bought "Happy Coats," a type of kimono, the Japanese version of lounge apparel. We drove along the Ginza, the main street in Tokyo, and to the metropolitan police station where Tetsuya worked. By now, I felt I had met all the police officers in the city.

As we drove from one place to another, Tetsuya told me much about Japanese life in 1970. Japanese traditions were still in vogue, as yet untouched by American influences. Many women still wore the kimono and not western clothing. Women did the cooking and domestic chores and the elders in the family were honored and respected. After the war, the economy had been revitalized, but many Japanese products were not available in Japan. They were exported instead. Some people in Tokyo protested this with particular regard to TV sets. They wanted to enjoy some of their own products.

Tetsuya also explained about the letter. Since last writing to me, he had changed his last name from Sawabe to Kohzuma, the name of his foster father. In Japan, if a man has no sons, he cannot pass his money or belongings to his heirs. Since Tetsuya's natural father had five sons, Tetsuya decided to let a childless man adopt him. This man Kohzuma, a friend of the family who had known Tetsuya since he was a young boy. It was good to have him educate me about Japan and Japanese life.

Japan is a land of contrasts between the old and new. Densely populated Tokyo has traffic and pollution problems, but the subway is efficient and clean. However, the subway is a place where traditional Japanese courtesy doesn't apply it is every man for himself. Most of the educated people in the city speak English and are friendly to the Americans but in the countryside, life is quite different. People are not in a hurry and some even stop to greet Americans. The economy is mainly agricultural. At the time, in Misawa, the locals were concerned about the recent base closures and how that would affect the economy.

They wanted the Americans to patronize their restaurants, rent their houses and so on.

The men dominated in Japan and the women were subservient and even did the heavy labor. I saw them digging ditches along the roadside while the men supervised. The Japanese taxi drivers showed no respect to women. The driver simply ignored me when I took a taxi, and I had to struggle with my luggage and packages. With this kind of attitude, it was easy to understand why so many American men liked Japan. They reigned supreme. However, in Tokyo the women did not seem quite so submissive. They work in offices, restaurants and department stores and walked alongside the men rather than behind them. They wore Western-style clothing instead of the clogs for footwear and kimonos. Their hair was cut in a short bob that was easily combed and styled. No decorations were placed in their hair.

On the whole, the Japanese people were polite and gracious, and very self-controlled at all times. One thing struck me more than anything else: The Japanese people seemed to lead disciplined lives with direction and purpose. In contrast, I felt rudderless and adrift, which leads me to excessive shopping. I felt a need to experience more of this discipline in my life and to learn more about the Japanese philosophy. The visit with my pen pal was too brief. At noon I needed to catch the train for Misawa. At the station, Tetsuya bought some packages of Japanese postcards to give to my friend and a special gift for me, a beautiful doll dressed in a red silk kimono which I will treasure all my life.

Now I had the opportunity to become more reflective about my own life. I tried to set aside time to meditate and to find peace in the tranquil gardens of nearby Towada National Park. The park contained a large crater lake surrounded by a primeval forest. The towering Hakkoda Mountains covered the southern area and from the summit of Mount Odake, I saw the Sea of Japan in the west and the Pacific Ocean in the east. Japan was a place of natural beauty. I felt this was a good place to find a sense of balance in my life and a true appreciation of nature. I would learn to pause in my journey, and take time to smell the cherry blossoms. I tried, but buying and accumulating things still dominated my life. I seemed to be trying to fill a void with the wrong things.

I lived on base and taught American students, which helped me feel at home. When I left the base, I experienced the Japanese language, food and customs in their fullness. I enjoyed visiting the dressmaker on a weekly basis to have her make me tailor-made clothes. My wardrobe in Japan was one of the best.

After living in Misawa for two years, I received a transfer to Yokosuka Navy Base, which is located south of Tokyo. Once again, I lived on base, so I was part of the American community. I made frequent trips to Tokyo and experienced the big city of Japan. There was so much to buy in Yokosuka and Tokyo. I couldn't find a dressmaker in Yokosuka, so I bought other things. The efficient but crowded subways reminded me of New York City. In spite of the crowds, I loved public transportation because I disliked driving.

While at Yokosuka, I was part of a Bible study group including three chaplains. This group helped me to understand the Bible in more depth. I longed for more. The chaplain suggested attending Fuller Seminary in Pasadena, California. I applied, was accepted and resigned from my teaching job in Japan. I had beautiful tailor-made clothes, kimonos and silk pillows to take back with me to California.

Again, I was leaving for a new place and experience and wishing to belong.

Chapter 4

Fuller Seminary

I went to Fuller Seminary in 1973 to obtain a deeper understanding of the Bible and to develop a closer relationship to God. I started with daily attendance at the seminary chapel. Attending chapel every day helped me understand the importance of prayer and scripture reading on a regular basis. The scripture readings gave me the fuel I needed for each day. The peacefulness of the chapel helped quiet me and meet the day in a more relaxed manner. I felt the presence of God in that chapel, especially when the sun came through the stained glass windows, the effect making the figure of Jesus a real presence among us. He seemed to come alive as the light of the world. The white lilies at the altar permeated the air with their sweet fragrance. The songs we sang, accompanied by the piano, gave our hearts the lift we needed for the day.

My theology classes helped me relate to God on a deeper level and to really delve into various verses in the Bible. Isaiah 5:8 is one that is an anchor for my soul. There are incidents in my life that I cannot understand because God's ways are not my ways. The friends I made at the seminary were people of substance. There was a Roman Catholic Priest Father Joe and David a Jewish Rabbi, both of whom helped me understand religious beliefs from an orientation different from mine. Roman Catholicism is not so different from my Lutheran background.

Father Joe even said to me, "You are more of a Catholic than you realize."

David showed me that the Old Testament of the Bible relates the history of the Jewish people and that is also part of Christianity. He said several times, "You are a Judeo-Christian." He helped see how the Old Testament and New Testament are related. When I read the Bible, I understood the connection which made Scripture so much more meaningful.

Another friend was Scott who introduced me to Dr. Carl Jung and told me I should attend the Jung Institute in Switzerland. He suggested that I become a Jungian analyst. This was all new to me, but he planted a seed. I wondered if this was a journey that God had in mind for me. It was enough to make me curious and to visit the Jung Institute in the future. Years later, I became a Jungian analyst, and it all started with Scott at Fuller Seminary. He never knew that I became a Jungian analyst, but God used his suggestion to start me on my real-life career path.

The marriage and family counseling classes at the seminary and at the Hollywood Center (by contract with the seminary) allowed me to be licensed in California for my future career as a counselor. I believe my courses helped me see and develop a healthier understanding of relationships and to encourage couples to look at communication regarding basic values in their relationship. II Corinthians 6:14 states, "Do not be unequally yoked with unbelievers," which took on a new meaning in working in pre-martial counseling. One of my fellow students in the marriage counseling program recommended that I see a Christian counselor after I admitted to him that I had headaches and difficulty concentrating on my reading. He gave me Dr. Venema's number and several days later, with fear and trepidation, I dialed the number. This was my first experience in counseling. On February 28, 1974, at 8:00 a.m. I had my first session with Dr. Venema. I started off by reading to him my problem of anxiety which I had written out. He said, "Tell me about it." After a while he said that I seemed more relaxed.

I said, "I don't trust people when I first meet them and I feel nervous."

"How do you feel around me?"

"Relaxed."

After several questions about my family background and my present relationship situation, he said, "You are a mystery to yourself. You tend to intellectualize things and block out your feelings. I don't think you are crazy but need to grow and this will help you as a counselor." I agreed to a second appointment the following week. I felt glad that I took the step to see a counselor, but I also felt very scared. I wanted the help, but I was resisting it. I prayed about getting the help and believe that the Lord wanted me to do this. I continued to see Dr. Venema for two and half years, until August 3, 1976.

I learned to relate more effectively to people and to develop close and trusting relationships. It was a long road, but the counseling gave me confidence and my trust in God became stronger. My personal counseling experience helped better understand and empathize with the clients I see. I know what it feels like to be on the hot seat.

Before school started, I found an apartment and had my household goods delivered. Oh horror! The crate was half empty upon arrival in Pasadena, but it was full when I saw it leave Japan! Where were my things?

The man who delivered the crate said, "This is all we received." Your things must have been stolen in Japan." "Don't worry, you will be reimbursed for your loss."

I was upset beyond repair. Tears flooded my eyes for weeks. How could this happen? A fellow student said this was a lesson for me because I had put too much of myself into things instead of focusing on God.

His words of wisdom did not comfort me, but instead only made me angry. The truth hurt, and I was not able at that point to hear that I had made my things my God.

I needed ego strengthening instead of being made aware of my weaknesses. It takes a strong ego to hear and accept the truth. I did wonder why God allowed this to happen to me. On a deeper level, the experience did penetrate my soul. My things were never found. All my tailor made clothes were never seen again. I was devastated, but the loss of belongings made me reflect on my habit of buying things when I feel lonely. I had friends at Fuller and enjoyed my classes. I belonged there, and the excessive buying stopped. This helped my budget and kept my weight in check. I no longer went shopping for enjoyment only for bare necessities.

The summer after my first year at Fuller a few of us were roped into applying for jobs at Sequoia National Park, where we had dual roles. We were part of a Christian ministry and conducted church services and Bible studies. My other job was to work in the cafeteria as a food server. It was hard work for little pay. A Catholic nun, Sister Ruth, was part of our group, and we became friends. She was like her namesake Ruth in the Old Testament who is loyal and true as a friend. We went on nature walks on our day off and talked about our relationship to God. "Pray without ceasing and believe that God answers prayer in His time" were words that I often heard from Sister Ruth. I learned to appreciate nature in the park. She stopped me and had me look at the wonder of a Sequoia tree. This giant made me realize how small I really am and how much I need God. We went on a bird walk in the hospital rock area and sat on a rock besides a waterfall.

The sound of the rushing water was soothing to us. It was cool there. The water was so clear, fresh and clean. We wondered when the swiftness of its flow would slow down, but its rapid pace never ceased its speed, which reminded me of my life a constant hustle and bustle.

The whiteness of the foaming water as it came rushing down off the rocks into the stream awed me.

The rocks had a shiny look as the water washed them on the way down. I wanted a shiny look too. Sister Ruth and I were energized as we took in the amazing sights of nature. She laid the foundation for my appreciation of nature. The walks in the park energized me and made the cafeteria job bearable. After the summer was over, I returned to Fuller, but the experiences with Sister Ruth lingered and helped me when I felt discouraged.

Before June 1976, I had to start making plans for a full-time job because my student days would soon be over, and I had to earn money to survive. Where would God lead me? I prayed and talked with trusted friends. I made an appointment with my advisor at Fuller to discuss my situation. I walked into his spacious and neatly decorated office. I sat down in a comfortable brown chair, and he sat at his desk.

I said, "Dr. Bower, I am considering returning back overseas for a job."

He looked at me wide-eyed and said, "Why would you do that? That is committing social suicide. It would be better for you to establish yourself in a community and develop relationships in America. The military environment is too transient, and you need to live in a more stable environment."

I listened to what I termed his sermon and replied, "But I cannot make enough money to survive in California."

He said, "Where is your trust in God's leading?"

"Perhaps it isn't there."

"I will pray for you to make the right decision."

I thanked him for his time and left, still confused.

I was offered a teaching job in California, but the pay and benefits did not match what I could make overseas. I was restless and wanted to leave California because three years was enough. I would not have the seminary as a support and I would be out in the world earning a living as a single person. I needed a good paying job with benefits, so with that idea in my mind I reapplied to the overseas schools. Job security was important to me and I was offered a job in Wurzburg, Germany, which I eagerly accepted.

I wonder how different my life would have been if I remained in California. I would not have seen nor lived in Germany, England, and Iceland. I would not have the government pension I now receive.

Fuller Seminary was a life changing experience. I had a neat and orderly apartment with only the things I really needed. It was here that the accumulation of things stopped for those three years because I had a lot of friends, and I felt spiritually at peace. In addition, my classes were stimulating and challenging, so my mind was active and creative. I liked attending chapel on a daily basis because the service gave me the boost I needed each day. I realized that being a student was a temporary situation, but it was so difficult to leave. I wanted my student days to last forever, but that is not reality. In my distorted reality, my next move to Germany would be Mecca. While in Germany, I took Scott's suggestion and visited the Jung Institute in Zurich, Switzerland, thinking that is where I would find my swans.

Chapter 5

Jung Institute in Switzerland

Once I settled in Germany, I took the train to Zurich instead of driving and then took a bus to the institute, which was away from the main train station. Once there, I talked to the grumpy Swiss secretary who did not seem to like Americans because they came without money. As soon as I let her know that I had a full-time job in Germany with a good salary she made an about face, and she became as sweet as apple pie with Swiss cream on top. She explained the program to me, and I said I would consider it. I did not want to jump into anything too quickly. It was a costly program and took many years. There was a summer intensive program with many interesting courses, including the interpretation of fairy tales. I attended four summers in a row before I applied as a full-time student. I could attend classes in the evening and on weekends and that would become my life for the next ten years. My analytical work was done on Saturday mornings. It was a wonderful life.

For the first trip to Zurich, I did not make any reservations as to where to stay for the night. I guess I was just excited to go to the institute. I walked to the nearby police station, and they recommended I stay at the Foyer Hottingen, which was a very simple hotel run by French nuns. It was inexpensive by Swiss standards and fortunately they had a room with a bed. I was grateful. The breakfast consisted of bread and butter and milk, coffee or tea. The bread was always fresh and tasty. I spent all of my Zurich time at the Foyer Hottingen. I enjoyed conversing with the nuns. One time, I had checked in and went to my class. As I left the class, I found out that my car had been impounded by the police. What was I to do? Another student told me to go to the police station and pay a fine. I did go to the police station, and they said I owed 300 Swiss Francs for speeding tickets. They did not have my address in Germany, so I was not aware that I had gotten speeding tickets. Oh goodness! I did not have that much money with me, and I needed to drive back to Germany. I thought of the nuns. Perhaps they would help me.

A policeman and I walked to the Foyer Hottingen and the nun at the desk exclaimed, "Frau Plesa what is the problem?" Her eyes were as big as saucers and her face turned as pale as the white part of her habit. The policeman explained that I needed 300 Swiss Francs to get my car. She went into the draw and pulled out 300 Swiss Francs. I sighed with relief and thanked her profusely. I could not believe that she trusted me. I told her that I would mail her a check the next day, which I did. The policeman with the money in his hand escorted me to my car and unlocked the block on the tire. I was so relieved to get into my car and drive back to Germany, watching my speed all the way back. When I told my principal the story, he was relieved that he did not have to bail me out of jail. He did not want to read in the newspaper, "American teacher jailed in Switzerland for speeding." That would not sit well with my students and their parents.

The Jung Institute is located in Kusnacht, just outside of Zurich. It was in a big stone building located on Lake Zurich. Our classes were held in that building. We could go to the boat house and just sit and watch the boats on the water. It was such a calming sight. The garden in front of the building had an assortment of beautiful flowers surrounding the benches where we could sit and eat our snacks. An apple tasted so good in that environment.

The best part for me was the friends I made at the institute. People came from Great Britain, Germany, Italy, Japan, Norway, Portugal, Spain, Sweden, and of course the United States. We would meet before and after class at the local cafés. One friend said, "We will never be in a place like this where we can bear our souls and be understood." She was right.

Several of my favorite classes were on the interpretation of fairy tales. Fairy tales can embody us and give us answers. Fairy tales with their powerful imagery help us access rich material from the collective unconscious so we can start on our journeys. My favorite fairy tale was "Snow White" because she was able to get help from the dwarfs, who represent outside forces when the family of origin could not give her the support she needed to function in life. Snow White's mother dies, and her stepmother is jealous of her and wants to destroy her. Her stepmother has her taken away to be killed but the kind woodsman releases her.

She finds help in the world outside of her home and marries her prince. The fairy tale helps those of us who come from dysfunctional homes or abusive homes to find others who can nurture us and helps us live fruitful lives. Fairy tales can make a powerful impact on our lives. They have filled a void in my life. Since my father was dead and my mother had been diagnosed with dementia, the people and classes at the institute were my mentors over the ten years that I attended. I felt that I belonged, and my friend Scott proved to be right that Jungian analysis was what I needed. My purchasing decreased just as it had when I attended Fuller Seminary but I knew that being a student was a temporary life. I had to move on once my studies were done and find a permanent residence.

I did not mind the three-hour drive to Zurich each weekend because

I looked forward to seeing my friends and being challenged by my classes. After taking a series of courses, we had to take six exams in various fields. I passed those exams and went on to the next level. I had to write a paper, so I chose to write on "The Ugly Duckling" and that made me realize that my swans were at the Jung Institute. I had to take additional courses and start to see analysts. That worked out well because there were many people in Germany who volunteered to be my clients. I attended a group supervision course in the evening. I would drive down after work, attend the course, spend the night, and arise early in the morning to be at work in Germany.

I felt fortunate to have a job as an assistant principal at an American School in Germany and a car to drive to Zurich. I felt so blessed.

Then, quite suddenly, in 1995, my life took a turn.

My principal decided to retire and a new principal came to the school. There were two of us as assistant principals.

My colleague was transferred to another school in Germany, so she had to leave in midyear. At the end of the year, I was informed that I was being transferred to Lakenheath High School in England. I was devastated most of all because I still had to finish my studies in Zurich. I would have to leave my clients and find new ones in England. I needed the job, and I could not afford to quit. My friends and analyst in Zurich were supportive and helped me reframe my thoughts. My analyst said, "Instead of driving, you can sit on a plane and relax." Public transportation is great in Zurich, so I could get around without a car. I wouldn't have to worry about speeding tickets. I made the move to England, and my new principal was supportive of my studies in Zurich. I flew to Zurich on weekends for the next two and a half years. I was fortunate to find analysands so I could continue my case studies. I had to take six more exams and passed all of them. I had to write a thesis and that was well received. I had to spend one summer working at a psychiatric hospital, and I was able to do that in Massachusetts where my sister lived. I stayed with her and completed the internship.

Even though the Jungian program was difficult, I was successful every step of the way exams, papers, thesis, case studies, and I felt that God was leading me through this journey.

Finally, after all the exams, courses, papers, and casework, I received a diploma in Jungian analysis in 1998.

Chapter 6

England

Hearing my friend Margaret read the Scriptures in church in her British accent, makes me think of my time in England. As I mentioned, I went to England reluctantly because I was still studying in Zurich and needed to complete my studies there. I was also tired of moving and realized that a new place brings new problems. The fact that it was not my choice to transfer, but instead was an administrative decision that I could not control, made it worse. However, in retrospect, England turned out to be a meaningful assignment on my life's journey.

I rented a lovely townhouse in West Row, which is a short distance from the base where I worked. A two-story red brick building with three bedrooms upstairs became my refuge for peace and relaxation. The downstairs area had a comfortable sitting room, a nice sized kitchen and a dining room to invite guests for lunch or dinner. A front lawn with red roses near the front door greeted me as I came home from work each day. Break-ins were a common occurrence, so a student helped organize my house so thieves would not see my TV or any electronic equipment they might be interested in stealing to trade for drugs. I never did have a break-in. I kept my curtains closed in the downstairs area. I did not have many valuables because I had sent my collections from Germany and Slovakia to storage in the United States.

Oh, the joy and peace of living in an uncluttered house! I would brighten it up by going to a Ma and Pa flower shop in a home where I purchased real roses, daisies, tulips, and carnations at a reasonable price. Each week I made my trip to the flower shop and decorated my house with real flowers. I learned to love flowers in my home in England. In addition, I could buy fresh carrots, beans and squash from the neighbors who had vegetable gardens. I was learning to live a healthy lifestyle in England.

Because I had many exams and papers to write before, I received my diploma in Jungian studies, most of my time was spent studying, seeing clients, and flying to Zurich twice a month or more, in addition, to working as an assistant principal at Lakenheath High School on base. Now I had to fly to Zurich instead of driving and, once off the plane, I had to depend on public transportation to get to class and case supervision. I often felt like quitting the whole program because I was exhausted. I often wonder how my colleagues made the commute from Sweden. I sacrificed physical, emotional and financial energy to become a Jungian analyst. I survived because of my faith in God, who provides what I need. In addition, the teachers and colleagues at the Jung Institute were supportive every step of the way.

An initial difficulty in England was finding clients for my case studies. I had to leave several clients behind in Germany and start anew in England. Leaving clients on short notice is not good for anyone. I did manage to find several clients who were teachers in the elementary school and that put me back on track for my case study exam. The teachers who were my analysts benefited because there was no other Jungian analyst in the Lakenheath area. I only charged $5.00 an hour, which was a bargain.

Finally, after all the exams and travel time, I received my diploma in February 1998 as one happy day. My analyst, Dr. Katerina Asper, attended graduation and her support was important to me because I did not have any family there. The graduation ceremony was held at the Jung Institute in Kusnacht. We received our diplomas at the ceremony and each of us gave a speech thanking others for their support and encouragement. I felt some sadness because I had no family there. My father was already dead, and my mother, who had dementia, was in a nursing home in the States. I was grateful that my colleagues and analyst were there because they had become my family. After the formal ceremony, we had refreshments and a chance to talk with the guests and say good bye to our colleagues. Later, one of my colleagues gave me a ride back to the hotel. I spent the evening alone. In the morning, I flew back to England. A part of my journey was complete.

When I returned to work on Monday morning, my principal presented me with a bouquet of flowers. I was touched by his kindness and thoughtfulness. I felt relieved and proud to have completed the program. Some of the teachers gave me cards and congratulated me. Now I devoted my time and energy to work and seeing England.

I did make time in my busy schedule to visit Ely Cathedral, an Anglican Cathedral of Romanesque architecture. It is fourteen miles northeast of Cambridge and eighty miles from London. It is a pleasant and easy drive from West Row. The Cathedral dates back to 1083. It is majestic. I was awed by its size.

Whenever I was there, I felt elevated in spirit. The high school held graduation ceremonies at Ely, which gave the graduates a taste of beauty. If heaven is going to be like Ely Cathedral, I want to put my reservation in now. I miss not having a cathedral in the United States where I live. Churches are beautiful, but a cathedral is awesome.

I also visited the local shops in Ely and each time I returned home with pleaded skirts, sweaters and blouses. I bought so many clothes I could wear a different outfit each day of the year. I like the English fashions and the clothes fit me well.

In addition to being the assistant principal at Lakenheath High

School, I was the dorm supervisor for 60 students. We had a travel budget, so I was able to take the students on trips and to various cultural events. One of the trips was to Dublin, Ireland. Once in Ireland we were greeted by a friendly tour guide. He took us to our hotel, where we ate a meal of Irish stew and soda bread. In the evening, the students learned to dance the Irish jig, which they found to be fun. We visited Trinity College and saw the statue of Molly Malone. Created by the Irish sculptor Jeanne Rynhart, it depicts her in traditional but revealing 17th century dress, hinting at her supposed part-time prostitution. She is also known as a fish monger. A traditional Irish ballad known as "Cockles and Mussels" says Molly was young and beautiful, selling her yield from a cart on the streets of Dublin. The song's final verse states that after dying of a fever she went on to haunt the city.

Aran sweaters were a big item that we purchased. The Aran sweater is handmade and so warm. I bought two white sweaters with different patterns. The cable stitch is a depiction of the fisherman's ropes and represents a wish for a fruitful day at sea. The diamond stitch reflects the small fields of the islands. They are great to wear during the winter in England.

We made weekend trips to London and saw the current plays. One we really enjoyed was Phantom of the Opera because the music is so moving. It touched me so deeply my whole body felt it. We visited Stratford Upon Avon to see Shakespeare's Romeo and Juliet performed. Live theater reaches me more than a movie. I empathize with the young lovers and their family disputes.

Because some of the dorm students came from Saudi Arabia, I visited the country for a week to meet with their parents. I was met at the airport by an American military member and put on the Abaya (black robe-like dress) and hijab (head scarf) that he had brought for me. I was covered from head to toe. I had to ride in the back of the vehicle, and had to be driven to every place because I am a woman. The airport in Riyadh is beautiful and peaceful. There are flowers all around and everything is very clean. Five times a day, I heard the call to prayer and the people stopped, knelt and prayed. It was something new to me.

In the market there were many things to buy, like jewelry, sheep skins, rugs and sandals.

There was something called a Saudi diamond, and I bought one of the stones and had it made into a ring in England. Everyone thought I had a very expensive diamond ring. The stones look real, and only a diamond expert would know the difference. The markets are a shopper's paradise. I also purchased my own black robe and head scarf as souvenirs. There are so many choices of scarves and robes so I had fun in a shop making a selection. The man was very patient with me and made helpful suggestions. There were many perfumes for sale in the market, and I bought Tea Rose. When I smelled it, it was as if I had a bouquet of roses in front of me. The perfume came in a lovely red velvet case. I also bought one in a blue velvet case, and it was gardenia. The perfumes were in small bottles, but the fragrance was potent. I have never visited a place as different as Saudi Arabia. Everything is so clean and orderly. There is peace and quiet in the city.

Once back in England, I continued to make trips to London and Ely. There was so much to see and do in England. I enjoy going to the pubs for a meal of cheese and bread. Dairy products in England are the best in the world. I loved the clotted cream, which is thick and made by indirectly heating full cream cow's milk using steam or a water bath, and then leaving it in shallow pans to cool slowly. During this time the cream content rises to the surface and forms clots or clouts. Nowhere else in the world can I find clotted cream with this taste.

The people are friendly and willing to talk and give advice, yet they respect your privacy. They seem to be a happy people with a great sense of humor. If I was feeling down, I could talk to a British friend and my mood would be uplifted.

It was in England, that I was introduced to Niceville, Florida. I was looking for a place to return to the States for leave and to eventually retire. A lady I worked with at the high school was from Destin, Florida, and she recommended that I go there. I was granted leave and during spring break, I flew to Northwest Florida and stayed at Eglin Air Force Base. My sister Betty met me there to help me look it over. She did all the driving because I was now an English driver on the opposite side of the road. I do not adjust well to driving changes, so I was grateful that my sister did the driving. We visited the University of West Florida. I applied to their doctoral program, was accepted, and moved to Florida in July, 1998, nineteen years after I had first tried to earn my doctorate before the death of my father.

One of the dorm students was from Niceville, so he told me where to live. His grandparents lived in Niceville and they let me stay with them until I found a house of my own. I commuted to the University of West Florida in Pensacola. Over the two-year period, I completed all my course work for the program. I arranged my schedule so I would not have to drive the 140 miles each day. That saved me time and gas. I enjoyed my studies and made several new friends. The best part was that I received an A in every course. Wow, I was proud of myself!

After two years of course work, I had to return to the overseas schools because I was out of money. I did work at three jobs, Taco Bell, substitute teaching, and counseling while taking courses, but I barely made it on my earnings. I was spending money as if the money would multiply by magic. I was out of touch with financial reality. I had to borrow money from my sister until I started working overseas again.

I returned to the Department of Defense Dependents School to finish out my education career. This time I was assigned to Iceland. I kept my house in Niceville and my friends agreed to watch over it while I was out of the States. I returned to the house in the summer and during Christmas break. It was great to have my own home.

As reluctant as I was to move to England, it turned out to be part of my life journey that would lead me to Niceville, Florida. I made good friends in England and visited London many times. England turned out to be far better than I anticipated. Now I was ready for my adventure in Iceland.

Chapter 7

The Dissertation and Doctorate

As a young child, I would tell people that I would obtain a doctoral degree even though I wasn't really sure what that meant. I had no idea how much time and energy it would take to achieve this dream. I was always a dreamer, but my dream was crushed when my father died, and my grief caused me to fail my preliminary examinations. At the funeral, I promised myself and my father that I would be Dr. Plesa someday. I realized that I had to be patient, which was difficult for me.

I was assigned to work in Iceland and started in August 2000. While in Iceland, I had to write my dissertation to complete the program and receive the degree. I arose at 4:00 each morning and worked on the dissertation. By 6:00 a.m., I had to get dressed and ready for work at the school. It was a difficult schedule, but I was determined to complete my dissertation and be awarded the doctoral degree in education. There were days when I did not want to get up early and work on the dissertation so I would have to make up for lost time on the weekends. In my mind, earning a doctoral degree would make me feel accomplished and give me a sense of belonging. I later realized that it gave me a place of status in the outer world, but the real belonging is in the inner world. While working on the dissertation, I missed seeing the natural beauty of Ireland. I wish I had built sitting by the waterfall into my schedule. It took me three years to write my dissertation and I was finally ready to defend it before my committee in Pensacola.

My neighbor was a pilot, so he was able to obtain a seat for me on the weekly plane that flew from Iceland to Jacksonville, Florida. The day I was supposed to fly, the plane was delayed. I was panicking, so I called the chairperson, Dr. Stout, and said that I thought I could still make the defense if the plane would leave the next day. We did fly the next day and we landed in Jacksonville. The pilot helped me gather my luggage and called a taxi to take me to the train station to travel to Niceville. As we arrived at the train station, I saw the train depart. My heart sank. There was only one train to Niceville, and I just missed it! I had to think quickly and asked the taxi driver to take me to the bus station. Once at the bus station I was able to get a bus to Tallahassee but that was still 220 miles from Pensacola.

Once in Tallahassee, I was informed that the bus to Ft. Walton Beach would go out the next morning, which is the time I was supposed to be in Pensacola. I called my friends the Wades in Niceville and they volunteered to drive the 150 miles to Tallahassee to pick me up and drive me to Niceville. They were the answer to my prayers. Once in Niceville, they gave me their car to drive to Pensacola to defend my dissertation. I drove the 70 miles from Niceville to Pensacola with tears streaming down my face. Who defends a dissertation after being up all night and driving while an emotional wreck?

I made it to Pensacola. The committee was very understanding of my situation, so I felt supported. After all the misses, I was elated to have the dissertation defense completed successfully. I planned to take the bus back to Jacksonville, but it never arrived, so my friends again drove me to Tallahassee, where I caught the bus to Jacksonville. Once in Jacksonville, I took a taxi to the airport. The pilot was already there, and he greeted me with a big smile. He could tell by my smile that the defense went well. He congratulated me. We boarded the plane and flew back to Iceland. The cold air in Iceland was a welcome reprieve from the heat in Florida. I did not attend graduation but happily accepted my diploma by mail.

This is how my life has been no celebrations; just move on. The doctorate was achieved but there was no celebration because my father had been dead for many years, and my mother had died two years before my doctorate was complete. I experienced no celebrations but was always driven to achieve something, although I never enjoyed my achievements. I just moved on to the next project as if anything I did was never enough. I went against tradition because I did not marry and have children. I did not fit into my family's mold, so I felt like I was coming up short. All my achievements did not seem to matter. I remember a neighbor lady telling my mother that my parents were wasting their money sending me to college because I would just get married and not use my education. The comment made me angry and hurt. I was more interested in an education than in getting married. I just wanted to be accepted for what I achieved and not what tradition dictated. I was invited to dress up in a Slovak costume and present myself at the Slovak embassy in Washington, D.C. Married women wear a certain bonnet that is different for single women. A lady at my church told me I could not wear the cepiec because I was single. I was upset. I called my cousin in Slovakia and she said, "Wear the cepiec." "Everyone wears it now." I wore it and my cousin affirmed me. I was glad I called her and that I followed my own way. Sometimes we have to break from tradition in order to develop ourselves. I seemed to march to my own drummer and struggled to belong.

I am completing the first draft of this memoir, and this time I am going to celebrate by taking a trip to Helen, Georgia. This is a city designed after towns in Bavaria, Germany. I look forward to being there and eating some German schnitzel at the Bodensee Restaurant. Buying things to clutter up my home will not be part of the celebration. It is uplifting to share my accomplishments with special people, but I had no one to share my happiness. It was a joyous time for me personally and yet a lonely time. I learned to live with the pain of loneliness, which is how I felt most of my life. One of my counselors admitted to me that he felt lonely too and that made me feel like I belonged in this world. I wasn't the only one who felt lonely. I never had a birthday party as a child or young person. For my sixteenth birthday, my mother gave me luggage instead of a birthday party. Most of my friends had sixteenth birthday parties, but I did not. My mother was a gift giver and not a party hostess. I would have preferred a party, but I didn't argue. I just accepted her gift. Once again with no birthday party and celebration I did not belong with other teenagers. That is how it was with the doctorate. I just accepted it with no celebration.

Home is where I can be a free spirit, where I can shed tears and work at my own pace. My home with its plants and collections reflects me.

Belonging makes home so important to me because that is a space and area where I can be a person.

The day after I returned to Iceland after defending my dissertation. I went to work at the high school, but this time, with the doctoral work finished, I didn't have to rise as early. The extra hours of sleep were welcome. Getting the doctorate was a life-long dream fulfilled. Now that the outer dream was fulfilled, I had to start on the inner work of praying and listening to God's direction for my life. Journaling and honoring my dreams are tools that have helped me travel on my inner journey. I also needed to experience nature on a regular basis. I would think about retiring from the schools and returning to my house in Florida. I prayed about the time to do it. I would have thirty years in the system and that pension would allow me to live in Florida. I could obtain other part-time jobs and set up a Jungian Analysis practice and finally put my training and education to work.

Chapter 8

Reflections on My Time in Iceland

In May 2000, I flew from sunny Florida to cold Iceland to scout out my new job.

The sleeveless top and shorts were exchanged for a sweater and long wool pants along with a coat, scarf and hat. As I stepped off the plane, a wave of cold air hit me like an avalanche coming down a snowbank. On the other hand, the unpolluted air filled my body and made my breathing feel as light as an air balloon. The wild wind howled like an owl and swept all in its path so I had to hold on to my hat. The trip did not deter me from returning to Iceland.

In July, Iceland would become my new home for four years as I became the assistant principal at A. T. Mahan High School at the Naval Training Station in Keflavik. As the plane approached the airport, I saw only brown and black patches of land. I began to question my decision. My immediate feeling was, "This will be dreary! What did I sign up for?"

I later discovered the unique beauty of Iceland, including the brightly colored roofs on the houses which contrasted with the brown treeless land. Iceland's natural environment grew on me over the months.

My first adventure off base occurred at The Blue Lagoon, a place I would visit frequently to relax. It was a geothermal spa located in a lava field near Grindavik. The sun's reflection made the water look blue, but it really was milky white. It was full of minerals, algae and silica. The silica when rubbed on my skin made it feel smooth and beautiful like a baby's. I even purchased a tube of silica mud to apply on a regular basis and had the smoothest skin of my life while in Iceland. The massage in the Blue Lagoon was the best I ever had. It was done in the water, which was warm, with temperatures around 99 to 102 degrees Fahrenheit. It was better than being in my bathtub.

There were swimming pools in just about every village and I swam at least twice a week in an outdoor pool in Vogar. I would be warm in the water and I could see the snow all around me. There were hardly any people there and I could swim and relax. The hot tub was next after my swim. The pool was Iceland's gift to me.

After the pool, the beach in Grindavik, surrounded by lava rocks and black sand, drew me to its shores on weary days. I sat and watched the waves move in and out with a natural rhythm that needed no human push buttons to keep them going. The sounds of the waves were steady, clear and audible like cymbals crashing in an orchestra. The sun above made them glisten as they splashed against the rocks that were cleansed with whiteness. As I practiced deep breathing the fresh air went through my body like a vacuum cleaner sucking out all the dust particles, allowing me to breathe freely. The air reminded me of my rosemary plant, which I kept in my apartment.

Iceland has many waterfalls and I fell in love with them. I liked the mesmerizing feeling of sitting by a waterfall. Skogafoss is a beautiful one that I selected to be my personal waterfall. I saw many rainbows there and standing close to it was overwhelming because it seemed so powerful as the water cascaded down, sounding like the steady beat of a drum. The mist dampened my clothes but felt cleansing and refreshing on my face. There was a legend that a chest with gold and treasures was behind the huge curtain of the waterfall, but I never found it.

It was placed there by Prasi Porolfsson, a Viking settler, around 900. He hid the treasure and said the first man who went there would find it. If I had found the gold, I would have quit my job as an assistant principal, because there was a crisis every day.

I needed a calmer and slower paced job.

The waterfalls drew me to them and inspired me to write.

I wrote this poem while watching the waterfalls.

Waterfall, waterfall, waterfall

Powerful and mighty like a roaring lion

Mother and protector as the Virgin Mary was of our Lord

Nourisher and purifier as the God of the Universe

Waterfall, waterfall, waterfall

Majestic and strong as a Sequoia tree

Natural and unencumbered as the sheep in the pasture

Waterfall, waterfall, waterfall

Your beauty, permeates my being and supplies my life energy

Your runner movement and baritone sound provide the rhythms of my life

I rest in peace knowing that you will exist beyond my finiteness.

Nature in Iceland seemed to draw out the poetic side of me. The words and thoughts flowed like a swiftly running river. As I neared my "farewell to Iceland time" over Labor Day weekend I toured Glacier Bay and was once again awed by God's natural beauty in Iceland. I felt that this pristine environment was truly God's creation. The various shapes of the glaciers reminded me of God's people all different sizes and shapes but each one unique in his beauty. The boat I rode wove in and out among the glaciers like a swimmer avoiding sharks. I kept wondering why it took me four years to visit Glacier Bay.

Being an assistant principal at A.T. Mahan High School was in such stark contrast to the peace and beauty of the outside world of Iceland. I was tense and tired each day and dreaded facing the tasks ahead of me. Suspending students for fighting, giving detention for being late to class and calling parents when students were disrespectful to teachers was not my idea of a job to enlighten our young people. I had to contend with irate parents on a daily basis, frustrated teachers each hour of the day and unruly students who hated school. Each day I waited to leave and go to the pool and beach to restore my sanity. There seemed to be extraordinarily little satisfaction in the actual work. The paycheck was the best part. However, some of the students at the school made the job worthwhile. I conducted a social skills group of nine boys, and we met once a week to help them adjust to the school environment. At the end of the year the boys presented me with nine red roses and a thank you card. I felt I had reached them and this made the time meaningful.

During my third year in Iceland, the principal became ill, so I was appointed acting principal of the high school for three months. It was a difficult job because I pleased no one and being the people pleaser that I am, I was frustrated. The experience made me realize that I did not want to be a principal and was elated when my principal returned to duty. An English teacher encouraged me to write poetry as a stress reliever. She even published my poems in the school poetry bulletin. I valued her friendship and encouragement. She was supportive of me and appreciated my style. One Saturday winter morning, I sat in my apartment, located on the base in Keflavik, and I just listened to the strong wind. I wrote down my reflections and observations and the result was the following poem, entitled, "Icelandic Wind."

I sit in my comfortable chair and listen
I listen and you speak
Everything around me hushes as you dominate. King Wind reigns supreme in Iceland
Your force is mighty and can be heard loudly inside the house
You are the mysterious and uninvited visitor
Everything inside silences to your presence

What message do you bring?
Good news, destruction, desolation, a clean sweep
If I listen carefully perhaps, I can decipher your message to me
The wind roars
"Quiet down and let me do my work."
In stillness and reflection,
The creative river is replenished
I force you to sit and hear my sound without acting
If your rhythm matches mine, the creative river will flow swiftly
If you oppose me, I will overcome you with my strength
Nature must be obeyed,
Icelanders have learned to flow with the forces of nature
I too can learn to adapt to the healing powers that nature freely
offers us

The teachers wanted me to be a strict disciplinarian and suspend students. I used my counselor skills with the students and had a great rapport with them. I did not fit the image of an assistant principal because I tried to reason with students to help them grow. The teachers saw me as a counselor and not an assistant principal. During my fourth year I was assigned a social skills class where all the problem students were placed, and I was supposed to fix them. I tried all kinds of creative activities, took the students on field trips, invited guest speakers and even made a video of the class. The students could not focus and remain on task for a whole sixty-minute class period. In addition to this class, I had lunch duty, gym duty, teacher visits and evaluations. Parent conferences, teacher bulletins, phone calls to community members, and building maintenance were part of my workday. I survived by the grace of God. I decided after four years as an assistant principal in Iceland that, I was done with education. I needed to help students in another way. I decided to retire in October 2004, after thirty years of working in education overseas.

Living in Iceland was a unique experience. I came closer to nature in this paradise when

I allowed myself to tap into the gifts around me. They strengthened me for each day of work.

I learned to appreciate nature in a new way while living in Iceland. This diminished the desire to buy material things and have an uncluttered apartment. I waved goodbye to Iceland and sang hello to Niceville. After thirty years overseas, I would make Niceville my home.

I knew I would have to do things to make myself belong in Niceville.

Chapter 9

Linden (Lipa) Tree

I am also looking for ways to connect to my Slovak heritage and belonging in Niceville where I have not met any Slovak people.

A book led me to the linden tree and many happy memories. "Slovakia: The Legend of the Linden," by Zuzana Palovic, arrived on April 30, 2020. I was so excited and read the entire book upon its arrival. Deda Jozefek (my grandfather) always talked about the linden (lipa) tree. He said that young children would have their pictures taken under the linden tree as a symbol of their connection to their Slovak roots. Both my sister and I have fond memories of the lipa leaves used for medicinal purposes. The tea would cure any stomach ailment, as it did for my niece when she visited Slovakia and my cousin gave her the tea. She remarked, "It really works." The linden tree with its heart-shaped leaves represents the warm heartedness of the Slovak people, whose country lies in the heart of Europe.

I had to plant a linden tree in front of my house to connect me to my grandfather and my Slovak roots. I started to look up information about the linden tree. I talked to a friend and he remembered attending a festival in Germany where the local people danced around it. My cousin said that they had a linden tree in New Jersey and her mother would dry the leaves and store them in a cotton pillowcase. Whenever someone had a stomachache, out would come the linden leaves and the tea was brewed for relief. The sweet-smelling flowers of the linden trees attract bees, and the honey is the product of the pollination process. Linden honey is medium sweet, with a woodsy flavor. It is light amber in color. I ordered linden honey from Amazon and quickly opened it to taste it. The sweetness went down so smoothly and a cough I was developing ceased. The blossoms are used to ease colds and flus. Extracts from its flowers and wood are used in lotions, creams and massage oils. It will be fun to make massage oil out of the linden flowers. If you look hard enough at the bark of a linden tree, you can see the face of a Celtic tree spirit.

I haven't seen one in mine yet, but I am getting ahead of the story. I started my search for a linden tree locally in Northwest Florida. I called several nurseries but they had never heard of the linden tree. I called Home Depot and the lady said, "I never heard of a linden tree but I will look it up." She found it and said, "I think it is a northern tree and would not grow here."

Disappointed, but not giving up because now I was obsessed, I called Lowes. The gentleman said, "I never heard of the linden tree, so we do not have it." He also said it would not grow in Florida because it was a northern climate tree.

Imagine living in a place where no one ever heard of the linden tree! The feeling of not belonging came up. I wondered if a tree, should I be able to find one, would survive in Northwest Florida. I know that sometimes transplants don't take root in new soil. I am a transplant from the north to the south, and rooting here was difficult. Would my tree so far from Slovakia survive in the south?

I refused to give up. I would find and plant a linden tree because this was my connection to my Slovak roots. When I know my roots and can have a symbolic representation of them, I can develop a sense of belonging in a new place. The linden tree would become my symbol of rootedness and belonging. I found Nature Hills online. They had an American Sentry linden tree, but it was expensive. I called Nature Hills and the gentleman said I was in zone 8 and the linden tree would grow in Northwest Florida. I could buy a warranty for the tree and get a new one if in a year this one did not thrive. I thanked him for the information. I then called my friend Ralph, expecting him to say, "No, it is too expensive, and it will not thrive in Florida." Instead, he was excited and encouraged me to buy one. I asked him to call Nature Hills and ask questions for me. He did and called me back to encourage me to buy the tree. He told me that they keep the trees in cold storage. With his encouragement, I called Nature Hills back and ordered the tree. My total with shipping and warranty was $115.50. I eagerly awaited the arrival of my linden tree and remembered my Deda showing me a picture of himself under a linden tree on his property in Slovakia. I wondered if my tree would be as big and attractive as Deda's. On May 7, 2020, the doorbell rang and I excitedly ran to the door to greet my linden tree. The FedEx man left the giant on my front porch. The cardboard carton was over six feet tall I really couldn't handle it by myself. I left it on the porch and asked my high school student helper to come over, unwrap it and plant it. He quickly arrived and opened the box. A tall, skinny and emaciated branch appeared. It wasn't as attractive as Deda's tree. Perhaps in time, with care, it would become beautiful. The roots were wrapped in brown paper. I wondered if this branch would survive. I had already purchased the topsoil and compost so all my helper had to do was dig the hole. The first hole he dug had too many roots winding through it, so that would not be good. He filled it in and started to dig a second hole. Suddenly, he noticed that the sprinkler pipe was there, so that would become a problem for the roots of the tree. He filled in the second hole and, frustrated, he tried a third area, and this one worked. We placed the tree in the hole and added the compost and topsoil. The next step was to surround it with mulch.

We then had to put stakes around it to give it supports. We watered the tree, and I continued to give it a drink each day because it must be kept moist for the first year. This little tree reminded me of myself trying to survive in a new area. Would I be able to tolerate the heat and humidity of Florida? I could go into an air-conditioned room, but my poor tree had to weather the heat and humidity. I had a nice house, but I missed having a basement where I could store things. Would the soil in Florida provide enough nourishment to my tree? The soil in Slovakia is much richer than the sandy soil here. I wondered about being accepted by Southerners because I was a Northerner. I wondered if the longleaf pines and the live oaks would be kind to my linden tree, or would the tree feel like it didn't belong.

I looked out my living room window and saw my linden tree branch I could hear Deda telling me about the tree. It was better than a bedtime story. Since Deda lived with us after my grandmother died, I would go into his room and sit in a chair by his brown desk. His desk is now in my house, and I can sit in front of it and think of Deda and the linden tree. His bright blue eyes would sparkle as he spoke of collecting linden leaves to be dried for tea. He missed drinking linden tea. I sat in the chair wide-eyed and said, "I want to taste the linden tea." He said, "We will have to take a trip to Slovakia to taste the real stuff," "I want to go to Slovakia and see the linden tree," I answered. Deda promised he would take me there. I could not wait to go.

When I see my linden branch, I feel connected to my Slovak roots. With my tree in front of my home, I think of Deda and know that I brought a little of Slovakia to me.

In addition to the linden tree, plants and flowers remind me of my father's garden, so I tried to create a garden with many plants.

Chapter 10

Plants: The Simple Life

One morning I had the insight that plants affect the way I live and give me a sense of belonging. I was struggling about what to write, so I left my writing desk, walked outside to my back patio and touched my basil plant, which gave me energy.

The sight of my plants provided the prompt I needed. The plants find their home on the red brick patio that spans across the back of my den and kitchen, surrounded by two additional rooms on each side, making the patio an enclosed area for privacy. I can sit in any room and look at my plants as well as sitting close to them on the patio. I marvel at their rapid growth. Sitting in the soil and taking in the sunshine on a daily basis is all they need to thrive. What a life! I envy them. Plants and trees seem to know how to live in the present. My two bright red geranium plants give color to the greenery of the basil and mint plants. A cup of tea made from the mint leaves gives me the zest I need for each day. Basil leaves, added to my salad or sandwich supply the perfect flavor. The pepper plant is tall and fruitful. It has given me three peppers to add to my salad. Two more peppers are waiting to be picked and sliced for a future meal. I planted the seeds so other pepper plants will sprout up. My fig tree, which I purchased as a small, emaciated looking plant, now sprawls across half my patio like a big green giant.

It has produced so many figs, and even eating two a day is not enough to keep up with its production, so I have shared ten figs with my friend Margaret. Watching my plants grow gives me the zest to improve my writing skills and to move ahead with my house cleaning.

Looking at my plants transports me back to childhood and adult memories. As a child I would draw flowers with bright colors. Tulips were my favorite because they were easy to draw. It seems as if tulips were on every drawing I made. The beautiful memories of tulips returned when, as an adult, I visited the tulip gardens in Holland. I dreamed of having a home surrounded by flowers. When I was a child, my father would take me to the Bronx Botanical Gardens and that was such a nice reprieve from the tall drab buildings that were visible to me on a daily basis. The apartment houses all gray lined the treeless dark streets of my neighborhood in the South Bronx. They glowered down on herds of people milling below them. One of the buildings had the numbers 632 painted on the front door window in big gold letters and that was significant because I spent the first thirteen years of my life in that building. The trips to the gardens became my dream world of beauty. They were created by the Torrey Botanical Society and Columbia University botanist Nathaniel Lord Britton and his wife Elizabeth Gertrude Britton, who were inspired to emulate the Royal Botanic Gardens in London. What a gift they gave to me! The gardens have 250 acres and over a million plants, which for me as a child was a world of its own. What a paradise for a child who loved flowers and plants!

A definition here is important to understanding how important gardens are to me and countless others. A garden is a planned space, usually outdoors, set aside for the display, cultivation or enjoyment of plants and other forms of nature, as an ideal for social or solitary human life. Gardens have a long history, and we can trace them back to the Babylonians. Homer tells of the Garden of Alcinous and the Romans were known for their gardens. We can learn about natural beauty and living from our ancestors.

I actually preferred the gardens to the Bronx Zoo, which was nearby. To see a red rose and take in its fragrance gave me a week of high spirits and was better than any vitamins. The Peggy Rockefeller Rose Garden will remain in my memory forever as a token of natural beauty on this earth because the sweet fragrance made me feel like I was in a fairy tale land. I miss the lilac trees, especially the lavender colored ones, because lavender (or purple) is one of my favorite colors, and it is also the color of royalty. There was even a serene cascade waterfall that I could sit in front of and dream of faraway places like Iceland. The gardens in England where I lived for three years reminded me of the Botanical Gardens in the Bronx. There were fifty gardens and plant collections. I could not see them all in one day. I would have to return several times, and I looked forward to each trip because the gardens reminded me of home.

A recent email I received from Viking advertised Garden Getaways to seven top gardens. They say, "Throughout the world, gardens are honored spaces where history, culture and art are revealed through the green and blossoming landscapes." Two of my favorite gardens are part of the tour the Keukenhof Gardens in Holland and the English gardens of Highclere Castle, Broughton Castle, Chavenage House and Highgrove House. I am tempted to take the trip just to see the other five, the Yuyuan Garden in China, the gardens at the Palace of Versailles in France, Italy's gardens, the Giverny gardens that inspired Monet, and the gardens of Monte Carlo. I am excited that the value of the garden is being considered and encouraged for people to see and enjoy.

A painting by a local artist of three pink roses sits by my computer, so I can see them as a symbol of beauty and transcendence. The realness of the rose painting and the different shades of pink remind me of my uniqueness in my writing. They sometimes have a voice that says, "Keep on writing, even though you feel discouraged."

Another garden lover who inspired my writing was Tasha Tudor, an American illustrator and writer of children's books. She was introduced to me by my friend Dr. Linda Smith and it was a match made in heaven. She had a house in Marlboro, Vermont, and her gardens were much bigger than mine. She had roses and peonies for bouquets, parrot tulips used for her paintings and delphiniums to enhance the view. She had an oak planted from an acorn just as my fig tree grew from a tiny single branch. Her japonica camellias exhibited their fluffy pompons of blushing flowers. She is quoted as saying, "I believe in making a big splash, so I plant shocking amounts of tulip bulbs." From the pictures in the book "Tasha Tudor's Garden," the garden may appear overgrown but to her it was paradise. She used everything in her garden for food, painting or decoration. Her garden inspires me to let mine grow as I like it.

The plants inspire me to reduce the complexity in my life and look to the simplicity of the plants for energy. Doing the mundane things, such as putting out the trash, washing dishes and sweeping the kitchen floor must be done, but they are tiring and sometimes diminish the creative spark. Taking a five-minute break to observe the plants seems to breathe into me the energy for the mundane tasks and creative experiences. The bright red geranium says, "Look at my color and visualize it for you to do your tasks." The flower speaks its truth. I need to heed its message and keep its bright redness as an image of creative flow. Oh, to have the life of a plant because it doesn't seem to be as encumbered as mine! I want to write, but all the other things like getting the mail, paying the bills, and grocery shopping get in the way. I need to focus on one thing at a time and look to the plants for that inspiration to focus. Their message to mc is, "Stay on task and look at us as we sit here on the patio in our silence." Oh, the wisdom of the simple life. I promise to listen, and when I forget, I will observe my plants to get back on track. I began to yearn to take a trip to New York City where I was born and feel energized by the city.

I needed to take a trip there.

Chapter 11

Thoughts of Home

Home in the evening of life is different from home in the dawn of life. According to James Hollis in Living Between Worlds p. 143, "Home is not a place but a journey, a process. The journey is our home. Our home is our journey. There is no place, to arrive where we know it all, where we are finally content. Inside each of us, there is a hunger, a burning desire to know, to explore." If our home is our journey, then growth, flow and development will become familiar companions. Is home a place, a building, or a journey? To me, it is all of that. Home now involves a smaller city with less traffic, less noise and more trees. Nature has become more important to me in my older age. I like to walk in the woods, where I encounter few people. I no longer need to be involved in big groups or events. That is too overwhelming. I want to focus in depth on just a few meaningful things a place or space where I can shed my persona and be myself. A house that is neat and organized with everything in place is at the start of my home journey. I can then reach out to the front area, with flowers, trees and of course my linden tree. The backyard, with its magnolia trees, fig tree and plants extends my home beyond the physical structure of my brick house. Beyond my yard is the golf course where I can hear voices and carts go by to remind me that there are still humans around. Home is where I feel safe and can think my own thoughts.

I feel safest in the addition I designed and added to my house. I have lots of bookshelves filled with books that I enjoy. I have a chair with a table and lamp. On the table sits my Bible and other prayer books. I start the day by reading my Bible and saying my prayers in that blue comfortable chair. This has become my ritual. I also have a desk with my computer and writing materials and that is where I do my writing. I feel at peace in this space and can be productive, with creative ideas for writing and living. I can think about my life journey and the meaning of my life. I am so grateful for this space that I have created for myself.

Home for me as a young person was having a bed in my own room where I could just sit and look out the window at the people passing by. I never had a room of my own until I started teaching at the age of 21. New York City, with its theater, museums and bright lights, was my home. I liked the hustle and bustle of the city because it gave me energy. The variety of people of all shapes, sizes and colors interested me. I enjoyed tasting food from the different cultures.

Japanese, Greek, Italian, Turkish, Spanish and Slovak food all appealed to my palate. I could walk down the street and buy a slice of freshly made pizza. Oh, what a treat that was! Riding the subway and taking the Staten Island Ferry were far better than driving a car. I could sit back and enjoy the sights while someone else did the driving. I could go to the public library and read books and magazines for free. I enjoyed taking the subway to the theater district to see a play. It was exciting to be on the set of a TV show and see how it was produced. While in high school I had the opportunity to appear in the audience of Dick Clark's Saturday night show. At one point, he sat right behind me and I was on cloud nine for a week. The excitement of a big city as home was great in my younger years, and I was proud to be a New Yorker. I thought the feeling of big city living would last forever, but something changed in the winter of 2020.

Chapter 12

New York Trip in 2020

A trip to New York always excites me because I think I am going home. I awoke at 3:00 a.m. to be ready for Todd my reliable taxi driver who would be arriving at 4:00 a.m. He was never late. I stood outside my front door at 3:55. ready for my ride to the airport. By 4:10, Todd had not arrived. Fear and anxiety gripped me. I called Todd's cell phone. All I heard was his voice mail message. I started to panic and wondered if I should drive my car to the airport and leave it there for a week. My hand shaking, I dialed Todd's other number.

Dave (Todd's partner) answered (a sigh of relief) and said, "I am in your driveway." "No" I said, "I am standing outside and no one is here."

Dave said, "I am on Sharon Drive."

Relieved and frustrated, I said, "I live on Golf Course Drive."

Dave said, "I will be there in five minutes."

Sure, enough five minutes later, Dave arrived. He had been sitting in the wrong driveway at 4:00 a.m. I am surprised that no one called the police or took out a gun.

Once on the plane, I found my seat and read "The Night Trilogy" by Ellie Wiesel. I wondered how the Jewish people could live with all that torture and the fear of the unknown. The book took the focus off of me and gave me greater empathy for the Jewish people. On approaching

Atlanta, the pilot announced that we could not go into Atlanta because of fog. We were going to Birmingham instead. No more was said. I started to panic. I wondered if I should get off in Birmingham, rent a car and drive back to Florida. I experienced the fear of the unknown, which is difficult for a person like me who likes to know all of the steps beforehand. Surprises are not my thing.

Once in Birmingham, we were informed that we would refuel and then travel back to Atlanta. I kept on reading to distract myself. I knew that I would miss my connecting flight to New York and the airport shuttle to the hotel. In the meantime, Delta did not even offer us a cup of water. We sat on the plane the whole time. I kept on reading my book. I thought to myself, I am not flying anymore. I was starting to appreciate the comfort of my Niceville home and the quiet area. Every little change or delay bothered me more in the evening of my life. I had become less flexible.

Upon arrival in Atlanta, I was directed to customer service to rebook my flight to New York, which was several gates away. I found it and waited in line. I then had the service agent, Wendell, rebook me on another flight to New York. He even traced my luggage, rerouting it to my new flight. I could not imagine being in New York City for a week without a change of clothes. Wendell showed me where to go for my rebooked flight. I had to go to another concourse and, surprisingly, I found the gate. The flight was delayed, as were so many flights that day. I sat down at the gate and called the shuttle company to rearrange another ride to New York. I continued to read my book until the flight was finally ready to board.

The hustle and bustle of travel are no longer exciting and energizing but instead stressful and tiring. We arrived safely in New York City, I went to find my luggage at the baggage claim. My bag was already there, and I took a deep breath, letting out the accumulated anxiety. Now I had clothes and underwear for the entire week. I found the airport shuttle that I had booked and was told that it would arrive in half an hour. When it did, the driver informed me that I was not on his list. I had to wait another half hour for the next shuttle. I was tired of standing but all they had available was a wheelchair and I said, "I will take it." The next shuttle came in half an hour, but it seemed like two hours. The excitement about being in New York City was beginning to wear thin. Was it worth all the hassle to go home?

I have difficulty when things do not go according to schedule. I guess I am not as flexible as I think I am. It is hard for me to go with the flow. I had the same difficulty when I was in Germany in 1990 when, at the end of the school year, I wanted to relax. I booked a boat tour down the Rhine. I missed the train which would take me to the start of the tour. It was downhill after that and the vision of relaxation disappeared.

Once in the shuttle, we had to go slowly because rush hour traffic had started. In addition, there were other passengers, so we had to drop them off. I was so exhausted and hungry. I thought for a moment, this is going to be my last trip to New York. I didn't have to put up with all this traffic in Niceville. I decided to change my thinking. Thanks to the limousine I booked, I was getting a tour of New York City with my ride to the hotel. I started to enjoy the sights and lights in Times Square. We finally arrived at my hotel the Doubletree on West 36th Street. I went to my room to unpack and get settled in. It took thirteen and a half hours to make the trip to New York. I better enjoy New York after all the delays because I kept thinking that a trip to the city should be fun and without any problems. I was living in a fantasy world. A trip to New York City is replete with delays that I seemed to forget. This was a wake-up call.

I had not eaten all day, so I went outside and found the nearest grocery store and bought a turkey and cheese sandwich. New York has the greatest variety of food places. They now have places that allow you to make your own salad, and one has at least twenty choices of what to put in it. I chose spinach, asparagus, tomatoes, grape leaves, sunflower seeds, olives, cheese, avocadoes, and green beans. These salad places seem to appear on every street, and I tried at least four of them, I ate well in New York City. I liked the variety of eating places and choices in New York but sometimes they were overwhelming. Niceville has a few eating places that I like, and I know what is on the menu, so that makes my decision easy. Decision making is difficult for me even when it comes to food choices. Too many options create anxiety and distract me from appropriate decision making. I tried Greek food and enjoyed the gyros I bought. I stopped at a Japanese restaurant and had an order of sushi, which is my favorite Japanese food. The raw fish wrapped in seaweed and dipped in soy sauce is mouth-watering.

After eating, I went to bed because I was exhausted from all the changes in the travel schedule. I moved slowly because my back hurt and my legs were tired. At the age of 78, New York city was too fast for me. This made me appreciate the slower pace of Niceville. All the lights and people and noise were too much for a quiet recluse.

After breakfast, I walked over to Good Morning America and went to the big window where Robin Roberts, Michael Strahan and George Stephanopoulos were on air. There were only a few of us by the window. Robin Roberts waved to us, which was exciting. I enjoy seeing TV personalities in person because it gives me the feeling that anyone can make it in America.

New York was the city of opportunity for me because I was able to obtain a good education and the diversity of people helped me to relate to all who are different from me. In my counseling practice I am able to relate to minorities because I grew up with so many different people in my neighborhood and in school. In the South Bronx, I was the token white kid and wondered why others were considered minorities. Once I left New York City, I encountered more white people and realized that they were in the majority in the country. How different that was from my New York City experience.

I attended the play 72 Immigrants and realized how the Mexicans in America fear deportation. I felt a sense of empathy for immigrants because it made me think about my grandparents who came to America from Slovakia. Perhaps they too feared deportation if they did something wrong. Oh, what a way to live in a new country! If my grandparents had not taken the risk, I would not be in America. I am grateful for their sense of adventure and willingness to take risks.

On my way back to the hotel, I found a jewelry store run by a man from Senegal, and he said he could find a stone to replace the missing one in my ring for $15. I was overjoyed because in Niceville I was told that I should throw the ring away since it was not worth fixing. I picked up my ring the next day, and it looked new. I can now wear it proudly. People in New York can repair things, while in Niceville they just discard them. In my home I would prefer to have things that have been repaired instead of buying new.

There are vendors on the streets and most of them are from Africa. The ones from Senegal speak French, so I could practice my high school French. It was good to hear them say how well I speak French. I always did well in foreign languages, and I like to practice my language skills. It is exciting to meet and talk with people from other countries, especially when I studied their language. So, when I meet a Russian, I can practice my Russian and the same with Japanese. I like to speak the few Korean words I learned at Korean restaurants. New York City, with such a variety of people, allows me to practice different languages and that is missing in Niceville where they hardly speak standard English. Because I speak several different languages and am at home in them, I feel like I belong when I can speak the language of the people I meet.

The next day, I visited Hudson Yards, which is a new development in the city. There is a walking park that was built over an elevated train.

The park walk had many high rise apartment buildings on either side of it, and all I could think was, I would not want to live here. I prefer my house in Niceville, where I can enter my backyard and admire my magnolia trees. I wondered why anyone would want to live in an expensive high rise that is clustered in with other buildings that block out the sun. I ended my walk on 23rd because there were stairs to the street below, and I was on my way to the Rachael Ray show on West 26th Street. I was the first one in line for the general audience. I waited in line for two hours on a cold and windy day. A lady from Australia came along and talked about Sydney. I have never been to Australia but was eager to learn about her homeland. She said that Sydney was a big and diverse city like New York. I thought to myself, Sydney would not be for me.

The taping for our group was at 2:30 p.m. and when the doors opened, we had to go through a security check. We sat in a big room until we were called to line up and proceed upstairs to the studio. We were assigned a seat, and I had a good one, with a view of the entire set. I was impressed with its three parts: the kitchen area on my left, the sitting area in the middle and the guest demonstration area on the right. Now, when I watch Rachael Ray on TV, I have a better view of the set. Before the show started, we were asked where we were from. A lady in front of me said she was from Florida, and the man who asked the question said, "No, you are from New York." She said she was from Florida by way of Boston. When I said I was from Florida he said, "Now, she is really Florida" "I guess I now sounded like a Floridian and not a New Yorker. I really have worked at losing my New York accent and have tried to develop non regional speech, which sounds more sophisticated. The comment made me feel like I had succeeded in changing my speech pattern, which I had worked at while attending the American Academy of Dramatic Arts in New York City during my younger days. There are people who do not like New Yorkers or the accent, so I worked on getting rid of it. It still frustrates me when people say I have a New York accent. I want to belong and sound like someone who speaks standard English.

The following day took me to Staten Island to visit Wagner College, my alma mater. I wanted to attend a college where I did not have to live at home but was afraid to go too far away. My family was dysfunctional, and I did not feel that I could succeed in college while living at home.

I graduated in 1963, and my parents and sister attended the ceremony. They were proud of me. I had not visited since 1970 and here it was 2020. I wanted to visit Wagner College because this is where I started to become my own person. I always enjoyed riding the Staten Island ferry and here was a chance to take that ride once more. The director of marketing, Patrick, met me at the ferry and drove me around campus. There were so many changes, although the view of New York harbor was still breathtaking. My former dorm, Parker Hall, was now faculty offices. I made many good friends in Parker Hall. We would encourage one another when we were discouraged about our studies.

I took a picture of my first room on the second floor where I experienced many pleasant days studying and talking with my roommate.

The daily chapel services are no longer conducted, which I think is a loss because attending chapel made my day while I was a student there. I looked at the stage where I played the part of Petra in Ibsen's Enemy of the People. The seats were a bright red color and far more comfortable than the ones in my day. I loved being in the drama club because I was made to feel like I had talent and that I belonged. I was even elected to the drama honor society, Alpha Psi Omega, and that made me proud. I actually joined the drama club because I did not make the basketball team and was very disappointed. Being in the drama club turned out to be a better fit for me. The last stop was to meet with Dr. Martin, the president of the college. His office had the most beautiful view of New York harbor. I wish I had that kind of view in my office. While I was a student, I was never invited to the president's office, so this invitation and encounter made me feel like I belonged. We discussed the progress of the college and particularly the drama department having students interning and graduates acting on Broadway. If those opportunities had been there when I was in the drama club, I might have had a different career.

More foreign students are now attending Wagner. I met a student from Iceland who is attending the school, and had the chance to exchange a few Icelandic phrases with him. He reminded me of my time in Iceland, with its beautiful waterfalls. I was impressed with how far my little college had come, and it made me proud to be a graduate.

Patrick took me to the ferry, and I returned to Manhattan. As we passed the Statue of Liberty, I felt proud to be an American. Yes, America is where I can achieve my dreams of higher education and be a free spirit in my home country. I can afford my own home and not have to listen to a landlady tell me when and how to clean.

Once off the ferry, I took the subway to 14th Street and went straight to the Donut Pub which has every kind of donut one could imagine. We don't have those delicious donuts in Niceville. I love baked goods and I miss the great bakeries of New York City. I could have bought twenty donuts, but I restrained myself and bought only two, a jelly and a chocolate with cream on top. I gobbled the donuts quickly so they would not become stale.

The donut shop was established in 1964, a year after I graduated, and I am glad because I would have been there on a regular basis. I would have spent my money on donuts and would have gained twenty pounds!

I walked a lot in New York City, which I used to enjoy, but this time while walking I found it hard to breathe. It was also hard to walk among so many people. What is so stifling here? I thought. There are no trees and fresh air just tall buildings that look like giants from another planet.

They block out the sunshine, light, and blue sky. I am grateful for all the trees that surround my house in Niceville. I would now appreciate them in a new way.

My cousin Pearl and her husband Freddy live in New Jersey. They drove to New York, picked me up and drove me to their house. My cousin Eddie, who lives about thirty miles away, drove up to visit. We had a lunch of pulled pork, fresh rolls, homemade coleslaw, pickles and olives.

We had lots of laughs talking about our younger days. We took pictures and compared them to pictures when we were young. When it was time to leave, Pearl and Freddy drove me back to Manhattan. They are two of my favorite cousins. I do miss family in the north since I have no family in Niceville. I do not want to spend a lot of time with family because I have different interests and I would rather do things alone. I enjoy going to the theater on my own. When I do things on my own, I can see the things I am interested in, I can move at my own pace. Doing things with family involves compromise and slowing down, which I have a hard time doing.

I attended a dream workshop for six continuing education units for my New York analytic license. The workshop kept my interest all day because the presenter gave clear explanations and good examples of dream interpretation. I met several interesting people and we chatted about the clients we are seeing as therapists. I learned how to look at the dreams of patients in more depth. It is difficult to find stimulating workshops in Florida relating to Jungian Analysis. They are non-existent. However, COVID-19 has sent many of us to Zoom, and I can enjoy workshops in the comfort of my Niceville home.

The last day in New York, I found a pizza place that charged $1.00 for a slice of pizza. Where else could I find such a bargain! The pizza, with its thick crust and melted cheese, hit the spot for me. After that I would only buy pizza from the $1.00 a slice store. I always look for bargains. Whenever I find one, I feel I use my resources appropriately. My home in Niceville was a bargain, and I am grateful for that. I also found a shoe shop that repaired my black shoes when others had told me to throw those shoes away. I was delighted with the new look of my old shoes. There is no shoe repair shop in or near Niceville. Oh, how the little things, like pizza for $1.00 and a shoe repair shop, make me happy.

I did not make it to the cemetery to visit the family plot. I normally do that, but this time I was too tired to make the journey to Brooklyn. I felt guilty, but rationalized that I had made the trip and paid my respects on all my previous trips. I guess I will meet my parents and others at the pearly gates. It makes me sad to go there because I think of our dysfunctional home, and I see my parents as tragic figures. They were talented but did not develop their talents. Instead, they worked at menial jobs just to survive. I do appreciate that they worked hard and provided food, shelter and clothing for me. I was never without the basic needs of life. I just wish that they could have developed their talents in art and music. If they were happy, I would have been a happy child instead of the sad sack I was most of the time. I shed so many tears that I could have kept the water reservoir going. I am a daughter trying to redeem my mother from not allowing herself to be creative and imaginative. She wanted to be a teacher and was studying, to do so but she was not able to complete her education, so I became a teacher to fulfill her dream.

My mother ended up being a cleaning lady. I think she resented that all her life. My mother could draw, and she crocheted beautiful things.

My father could sing and play the accordion. Maybe, I really wanted to avoid the flood of sad memories regarding my parents, so I chose not to make the cemetery trip.

The trip back to Niceville had its delays as well. The shuttle came later than scheduled. While I was waiting for it, the hotel person gave me a chocolate chip cookie and a bottle of water. He was so kind.

Once at the airport, I checked my bag and it weighed 49 pounds the limit is 50! I was so relieved that my bag, with all my purchases, made the weight limit. The flight to Atlanta was on time and it was not a full flight, so I had lots of room. What a relief! The flight to Ft. Walton Beach was delayed three hours because the plane had a fuel leak and another plane had to be cleaned and brought in. While we were waiting I met a few friendly people, so the time went quickly. While waiting, I opened my backpack and the zipper broke. Oh well… I need a new backpack now, because no one will repair this one in Niceville.

We finally boarded the plane and again, there was lots of room to stretch out. This was another thirteen-hour trip because of the delay.

Once at home, I unpacked, showered and went to bed early. I was so happy to sleep in my own bed. New York is no longer home. It is a great place to visit but the pace is too fast for me. With all the museums, plays, art galleries, street vendors and food places, it is a cultural mecca for the young, but Niceville is a better pace for retired people. COVID-19 changed New York City. I visited and left before the pandemic hit and experienced New York as it no longer is. The plays have shut down, as have the restaurants. I now enjoy the peace and quiet of Niceville, which is my home now.

I am not sure I will make another trip to New York City.

Chapter 13

A Place to Park

I hope the ringing phone means Sophia is calling to cancel her visit.

"Hello Sophia." You are on your way to my house? Drive carefully and I look forward to our tea time." She invites herself over so she can criticize me and make herself look good. I feel like a wet, rung-out mop when I am around her. I wish I had the courage to tell her not to come but instead I put on a welcoming smile.

Since Sophia lives two hours away, I have time to clear the table of mail and unread magazines for a light lunch. I will have to steel myself against Sophia's remarks about my excessive acquisitions and cluttered rooms.

After the call, I take a few minutes to sit and meditate in my Chinese rocking chair, surrounded by boxes of books, dishes, crystal, and dolls. Even after a year in Niceville, I have to walk over and around piles of books, papers, and clothes to move from one corner to another.

Sophia retired a year earlier than I did. She will criticize my lack of progress. I can hear her now. I know she will say, "Zuzana... I can't believe how much stuff you have acquired. Did you think that you could afford a ten-room castle to display all your treasures purchased overseas?" Sophia will not hesitate to share her unsolicited words of wisdom.

I treasure my hundreds of books, my doll collection, and my twelve sets of English Bone China. Sophia doesn't understand how much these possessions mean to me because Sophia has a son and daughter.

It's an interesting question: How much does the outer home affect one's inner peace? The piles of books, blankets, pillows and clothes strewn all over the house lead me to take a nap or watch television. I used to be so organized as a young person. Now a dark cloud looms over me as I look around each room. My thoughts are that I will never get this house in order. I have created a mess with all my buying. My negative thoughts make me feel tired and lacking in energy. It is difficult to even open one box and sort the collection of towels and tablecloths. I feel like just sitting and staring into space.

I remember spending summer vacations arranging and organizing my mother's house. I placed all her skeins of wool in boxes according to color and labeled each box. All the red wool was in one box and the blue wool in a separate one. I placed the boxes on a shelf with the labels visible so one could see what was inside. I arranged my mother's cookbooks and knitting books by subject and in alphabetical order. It was so easy to find the book she needed. Being organized, with everything in its place, was my pride and joy. Something has changed within me and has led to outer disorganization and clutter. When I want a book I cannot find, I order another one. Now I have duplicates of several books. My inner loneliness and seeking for my place in the sun led me to start buying things to fill the emptiness I feel. I went overseas to escape my family but instead the inner turmoil followed me. I needed to be among people who supported me and not in foreign cultures. I left home physically but carried my inner turmoil to distant lands. I felt so empty inside and stuffed food into me to feel better. I was a bottomless pit that would never be filled. My head, back and legs ached. My head felt like a redwood log. Memories of my father sitting at a bar with his shoulders slumped and his gray curly head bent over his glass of beer return. He turned to alcohol and I to shopping for relief from the pain of living. Allowing my own journey and responding to the values of the collective society around me cause me great anxiety. Avoidance of the conflict leads me to sleep and sleep. My mother showered me with gifts, but what I really needed from her was support and approval. I always felt like a bad kid because I could never meet with my mother's approval. If I dusted furniture, she would find the place I missed. I rarely heard any positive comments from her. I so yearned for her approval of me as a child.

I remember her saying, "If you can't do it perfectly, don't do it at all." Nothing I did was good enough. Perhaps my father felt the same. She never seemed to appreciate anything he did and complained about everything we did not have. She wanted my father to own and drive a car like her friend's husbands, but we did not have a car. My father defended her by saying, "She is a hard worker." She made more money than he did. My reality of life is distorted in that I want everything to be in order and peaceful. Life is full of ups and downs, and I have difficulty dealing with the roller coaster of life. My father died at the age of 71, and perhaps he found a slice of peace through death. I vowed not to let alcohol become my addiction because of his life. I substituted shopping and collecting as my addiction. As I look at all my clutter, I better understand why it is so hard to control addictions. Each day I say I will not buy another thing, and then I see a book or dress and rush to purchase it. My father would say each day that he would stop drinking, but by noon he was drunk.

I turn my gaze to the magnolia trees that surround my light pink brick ranch home. The grounds are interspersed with islands of green bushes and flowering impatiens. The tapestry-like lawns with their mixtures of St. Augustine, Bermuda and Centipede grasses, weave in and around the majestic trees. A squirrel chips away at a pine cone on the roof while the tree branches dance to the melody that the birds sing.

The fresh air allows me to breathe deeply and expand my lungs. The air is tinged with fresh cut grass. The soothing songs of the birds are like the lullabies I wish I had heard as a child. My ginger plants have the fragrance of linden sweet honey. Their white blossoms and green leaves welcome neighbors outside of my front door. A bit of paradise exists on Golf Course Drive, with its fourteen buildings, each one bearing the unique stamp of its occupants. Some are big, others small, some are traditional and some are modern. The bright green surroundings and the quiet are a pleasant reprieve from the noise of foreign countries. I disliked living in rented apartments and houses because the landlords felt that they could come by at any time. I felt that I had no privacy in rented places, so I am grateful for my house. Even the recent hurricanes have not left permanent scars.

Niceville is a nice, quiet, safe place to live and so different from my roots. I'm a transplant to the South, drawn by fantasies about spending the day on the verandah (which is actually a patio) in comfort and ease. After thirty years of traveling and living in Japan, Germany, England, and Iceland. I have found my Mecca in Niceville, located near a U.S. Air Force base, and inhabited by active duty and retired military personnel. The outward tranquility I long for is here, but something inside of me is in a state of malaise. The old questions of will I belong here and will I be heard in this community keeps arising. As a child, I did not have many things. I did not even have my own room until I was thirteen years old and then I shared a bedroom with my sister. I was twenty-one years old when I finally had my own bedroom apartment in Denver. Having my own bedroom was special because I could write and daydream in my own space. Going overseas enabled me to see new things that I could not afford as a child but now, as a working adult, I could purchase dishes, crystal, dolls, stuffed animals, a grandfather clock and curio cabinet. I was lonely overseas, so I filled my emptiness with beautiful things. I did not give thought to where I would place my purchases or how they would fit into my apartment. I just shopped, which gave me a temporary high. Now that I have all these beautiful things, it is difficult to get rid of them, but they no longer fit into my lifestyle. I want a neat and organized house, yet I cannot let go of my purchases from all over the world. All the self-help decluttering books and suggestions do not seem to help. I have to find my own way to let go. The buying started after my father died and if I let go of my things I let go of my father.

I cannot let go of my father.

It is so quiet in this neighborhood and even quieter in the house. This quiet and contemplative phase is needed at this time of my life. Looking at other homes and places on the internet diverts me from dealing with the present. Bigger homes in new places give me a false sense of hope. Running from my present place seems to be my way of handling life. Niceville is my home and I need to focus on my reality and that is to declutter. Making my home neat and uncluttered is my goal. Sophia, said that I should research the demographics of a place before settling there, but her process is void of feelings and when I first saw Niceville, it felt right.

I've had no experience in choosing a "place to park my car." An English teacher who wrote stories in my spare time, I looked forward to having the time to write; but I haven't written anything of substance in the last year. My mind is full of saw dust and needs to be cleared to let the creative ideas leap forward. My living space full of partially unpacked boxes filled with knick-knacks and ceramics reminds me of all my incomplete efforts: a piece here and a piece there with no Ariadne thread to connect them. I really have tried to put my energy into unpacking and arranging my quarters, but after a year, only one room is in order, and the others are a mess. A woman's home is her castle, and mine does not seem to have enough room for everything I own.

I will never have enough room because I cannot part with anything.

I think I might be able to use these things in the future.

I also like to be independent of others, so if I have everything I need right at home

I don't even have to leave the house for what I need.

I like to have everything under my control.

I become anxious when there are events and activities that I cannot control.

It is this need to have a voice which I didn't have as a child.

It is again the wrong medicine because when you have too much you actually lose control.

I have lots of books so I don't have to go to the library for reading material.

I tend to isolate myself with my things.

I prefer just staying at home by myself.

I can do what I want when I want.

I buy and buy but do not discard the old. New dresses hang beside high school dresses.

I have difficulty parting with my things because there are many good memories connected with my worldly acquisitions. Hundreds of boxes stuffed with curtains, towels and table linens fill two bedrooms so completely entry is impossible. I can only stand in the doorway and look at the wall-to-wall boxes lining every inch of space.

I don't know where to start, so I do nothing.

I think of getting help, but I resist because hired workers want to tell you what to discard. My things are not valued by other people and they are ready to toss my treasured old newspapers. I stand like a wooden solider watching someone take over my things.

Why do I hold on to things that are not memories? Holding on to things that are not memories keeps me from moving forward. I am afraid of moving ahead. What would I do or be without my clutter? Having a lot of things gives me the identity of being rich.

I can give things away to people to fill their needs and to fill my need to share what I have. People ask me for clothes, boxes, towels and, vases. At times I feel taken advantage of but I give away what people ask of me. I keep things to give away, so I don't have to say no. It is difficult to say no to people because they will be upset with me. If I didn't do what my mother wanted when she wanted, she would refuse to speak to me. I was devastated when she shut me off for weeks at a time. She made me feel like a disobedient child.

I can give away my clutter and make people happy so they will not shut me out. If I have no clutter, what can I give away? My mother was always giving things away. I observed that as a child and people would show me jewelry that she had given them. I felt envious because I wanted the jewelry and clothes that she had given to them.

Too soon, the doorbell rings. I paste on a smile and open the door. Sophia, tall and slender with light brown hair, exudes a lot of energy. I greet her, pretending to have as much energy as she does.

As Sophia looks around, I can tell from her facial expression what she thinks, although she doesn't say a word. Embarrassed, I rush to explain away the piles of boxes, books and cherished collections.

"I've been so busy attending church, volunteering at the local hospital, writing children's stories, and teaching American Literature at the local college." I just haven't had time to finish unpacking."

Sophia looks around the room again. "My things were unpacked in a few days, "she says, "and I still find time to enjoy things." She shakes her head as if throwing off unpleasant thoughts. "Never mind that. Your house is so cute. You will have to show me around."

I feel a sick, churning in my stomach and respond, "Oh, Sophia, I still have to put my doll collection in order and my twelve sets of English Bone China are still in boxes."

As I usher her through the rooms, she says, "Zuzana, I cannot believe how little you have put away! What have you been doing?"

"It's three bedrooms, but it's not big enough for all my collections. I'm taking my time, and I do a little each day."

"At your rate, death will arrive before everything is in order," Sophia says.

I feel the temperature rising in my face, but I maintain a pasted-on smile. Sophia takes out her cell phone and says, "Zuzana. I am going to take pictures of your rooms and send them to you. When you've finished unpacking, you can then see the before and after."

This is more than I can bear. "Please Sophia. No pictures. I don't need to be reminded of how messy all this is." Sophia puts her phone away. We sit down to tea.

Sophia says, "A decorator could do wonders with your house. My decorator would be perfect for this mess."

"I don't need a decorator because I can fix this up on my own even if it takes time. I am in no rush."

With a huff, Sophia puts away the card with the decorator's name and number. She continues, "You cannot keep living this way. It will depress you," I feel tension throughout my body, yet I say nothing. I avoid conflict with my silence about how I feel regarding her advice and instead I thank her.

"One of the volunteers at the hospital where I am volunteering said something unflattering about how a third volunteer dresses, and I told her how catty she was," Sophia says. "Clothes are so expensive where I live. I cannot find a decent dress for a reasonable price," Yet she hires a decorator but will not buy herself an expensive dress. My headache is going to need two aspirin after listening to Sophia talk about all these things that concern her so deeply. After several hours of my listening, Sophia finally leaves.

Relieved, I cry and pray at the same time. However, Sophia's criticism helps me to examine what I am doing with all these things. I don't accept her help because she, like my mother, will be too critical of me. It seems that the women in my life want to tell me how to dress and how to talk. They seem to want to make me over instead of allowing me to be me. I need to feel affirmed, not criticized. It would be nice to hear, "You have good taste with all these beautiful things." I need someone to just trash the things I want to get rid of and to place things where I want to place them.

I think about coastal living to help myself feel better.

Sparkling, breezy, emerald-colored waters contrast with tiny white pearls of sand on the beaches, inviting all to participate in northwest Florida's coastal living. The in and out movement of the waves parallels the creative process within the artist in me. Cool breezes keep the sweat off my brow and temper the warm rays of the sun while I reflect on the next step in my individual journey. Coastal living is where I can paint, sing, dance; where my creative juices can flow freely while savoring fresh shrimp, salmon, mullet or catfish. Where else can I walk up to a shrimp boat and purchase a fresh catch? The cleaning of the shrimp and their smell on my hands leads me to a greater appreciation of the meal.

Living near water is a meditative experience because water is cleansing and symbolic of what exists in the depths of our being. As I approach the water, answers to my human questions come to the surface. If I pay attention to what bubbles up inside, a sense of peace envelopes me. A barefoot walk along the beach, with each footstep feeling the soft cool sand as if it were an air mattress, provides the tranquility that my body and mind need for nourishment. The mist of the gulf waters brightens my skin and penetrates even deeper to my inner river. Water, beaches and trees are healing for my soul, and my medicine is found in the coastal areas of northwest Florida. I need to connect with nature at least once a week for healing and energy.

Sophia calls me a week later and asks, "How much progress have you made?"

I say, "I have emptied and put away five boxes."

Sophia replies, "That is better than nothing."

I feel good about reporting my progress to Sophia. I realize she wants to help and I can let her do that. In fact, it helps me to be accountable to someone. Being able to tell Sophia about my progress is a motivator for me.

The ringing doorbell announces the new morning. Matthew, a stocky blond-haired man, appears at the door, ready to repair my computer. Matthew is retired from the Air Force and now runs his own computer business. Most of the people I've met are retired from the Air Force and have chosen to remain in Niceville. I'd spent thirty years working for the military and one of the draws of Niceville is maintaining that connection.

Looking around the room, he says, "I see you're having trouble getting all organized." He says it as a quiet observation, almost like a doctor diagnosing a patient. Unlike Sophia, he does not seem to be judging me.

"Yes," I say, "It is just so overwhelming."

He nods, "It took us twelve years, but we finally have everything in order." I feel such a sense of relief I almost laugh. "I can't live with this mess for twelve years," I say, "I'll probably be dead by then."

Matthew's blue eyes scan the room. He noticed the one hundred trays of slides on one shelf and the two hundred photo albums on others. He says, "We put our slides and photos on CD's and that cleared out a lot of space; my mother could do that for you for a small fee." Feeling a surge of energy back in my life, I jump at the opportunity. Later that day, Matthew's mother, Mary Ann, a short but energetic woman who is clearly the source of Matthew's blond coloring, appears. She is dressed in slacks and a blouse to pick up the slide trays. One corner is now available to be filled with the papers, strewn all over the floor. Matthew and Mary Ann inspired me to continue sorting and discarding. I have taken the first big step to organizing the house.

With some of my boxes unpacked, I look around and draw energy from my unique displays of dishes, dolls and crystal. They bring back happy memories of my overseas experiences. Misawa, Japan was where I first ate sushi in a restaurant, with the Japanese class I was taking. We all dressed in kimonos and tried to fit in with Japanese culture. My pale-yellow kimono fits comfortably. It still hangs in my closet. I continue to eat sushi and seaweed rolled around rice. Sushi and seaweed hit the spot better than chocolate chip cookies. Rice isn't as tasty as in Japan because most American restaurants use regular rice instead of sticky rice. Learning to use chop sticks was an art I never mastered, although I tried. Perhaps being left-handed makes it more difficult to manage the chop sticks.

Slowly, I realize that I will make my nest right here in Niceville. Niceville is convenient, safe and quiet. Quiet and slowness are now my speed.

Reading Julia Cameron's book; <u>The Artist's Way: A Spiritual Path to Higher Creativity</u>, helped me realize that buying things and filling my house to the point of it being cluttered was blocking my creativity. All I wanted to do is sit and vegetate or go shopping for more things. It was the wrong medicine, and it took a long time to come to that realization. Her suggestion of morning pages that is, writing three pages every morning is the primary tool of creative recovery because we put on paper the things that block us. We unlock ourselves to allow the creativity in us to flow. I have to come to terms with the fact that uncluttering and organizing is an ongoing process, and I have to get in step with that process. One corner at a time needs to be put in order and then looked at frequently for reassurance that progress is being made. Trying to declutter too much at one time can have a negative outcome.

Baby steps is what works better to get rid of accumulation. I have become aware that my energy level has slowed down, so I have to make some choices. I realize that I can only do one project a day before I become tired. I made the decision to make my writing a priority and my decluttering a secondary project. I am writing on Monday through Thursday at the beginning of the day when my mind is most creative, and my energy is high. Friday and Saturday are the two days I will devote to decluttering. I am writing chapters for my memoir and I have decluttered my living room and dining room.

I look at the two rooms that are in order and sit in them to keep me motivated to complete the other rooms in the house. Writing and decluttering are keeping me going. I will send Sophia pictures when I am finished because her criticism sent me on the path to putting my house in order.

Chapter 14

Projections

A peek into my one car garage known as The Doll House; one catches a glimpse of all the dolls I have collected. All of my dolls are packed into the garage house. Some are on the built in shelves and others still in boxes are packed in the lower cabinets where they sleep in peace. The shelf dolls are arranged by country or theme. The Korean and Japanese dolls line four shelves. The Slovak dolls have their own shelves because there are so many in their village costumes. My German dolls occupy another shelf. I have only one Icelandic doll because I gave one away to the doll museum. The remainder of the dolls are Native American, Black, babies, and Southern Belles. There is diversity in the doll house and they all seem to get along. I never hear any noise from the doll house. The "Gone with the Wind" dolls have a shelf of their own with Scarlett, Rhett and Mammie. There are five Scarlett dolls each one dressed according to the makers vision of Scarlett. My 15 bride dolls are on a shelf under the one window in the house. They come in all sizes and shapes. There is a Princess Diana bride and a Sarah Ferguson bride standing side by side as if competing for an audience.

I have five sets of dinnerware. One set is blue, one is white, one has yellow flowers, and the other two have flowers with many bright colors. I have already given a dinnerware set to both my niece and nephew as wedding presents. I have given my sister one set of Christmas dinnerware but still have one for myself. The dishes are from England, Germany and Japan. The dinnerware I use on a daily basis is American. I have to find others for the dinnerware that I still have packed into my house.

Books are everywhere. I love to read and I have books in three different rooms. I will never read all of them in my life time. I even had an additional bookcase constructed and it is filled with books. I have books on Jungian Analysis, Novels, Slovak, German and French language books, Art books and Cook books.

I didn't connect with my mother and the feminine. Is the excessive doll collecting a way to recognize the feminine in me? Is it to give the feminine a voice? Am I trying to heal my mother-child relationship ? Are the dolls my children to which I never gave birth ? Are the dolls people to whom I can speak and they will not speak back or criticize me?. They allow me to belong. They just look at me. Some smile, some cry and others just stare into space. The dolls are a part of me and it is difficult to part with them.

One night when I was attending a Zoom class on the psych I learned a new concept: Projection. Projection is a defense mechanism in which the human ego defends itself against unconscious impulses or qualities. It is a defense mechanism that occurs when a conflict arises between the unconscious feelings and conscious beliefs. In order to subdue this conflict, one attributes these feelings to someone or something else. One transfers ownership of troubling feelings to some external source. Am I fooling myself by projecting my feelings onto things.

Jung defined projection as an unconscious, unperceived and unintentional transfer of subjective psychic elements onto an outer object. One sees in this object something that is not there, or if there, only to a small degree. Jung speaks of a hook in the object on which one hangs a coat on a coat hook. That night I awoke with an insight. Am I fooling myself by projecting my feelings onto things. Do I pretend to be a hostess with all my dishes? Do I want to appear to be a social butterfly when I am a recluse. What a gift!

I made a connection between excessive buying and projection. It was brought up that we can project onto things such as books, clothes and dolls. Yes, I have put too much into things. I was trying to get blood out of a stone What was I trying to project onto all the books I have in my library. Was I so unsure of my intellectual ability that collecting books would make me appear smart even if I had not read all the books I purchased and kept in my library.

My awareness has brought me to the point of starting to detach from some of my things and give them away. That is a freeing feeling but it has to be done at my own pace and my own awareness. I cannot have other people come and help me because they do not have the same attachments that I have. I also have a collection of National Geographic dating back to 1937 which my father started. I am trying to give away my National Geographic but I have not found any takers. I even contacted an elementary school but they have no room for magazines. I thought the children would enjoy the pictures. There must be someone out there who will benefit from the magazines so I wait for that special person to cross my path.

I am a collector and not a hoarder so I have to decrease my collections and give them to people who will appreciate them. My dolls will go to doll collectors and little girls who love dolls. My dinnerware sets will go to my sister, nephew, niece. and special friends. They appreciate good quality dinnerware.

The awareness took a long time but I am glad that the light bulb finally came on. Now I am in the process of slowly dispersing my collections to people who appreciate and use them. I feel sad that I put so much time, energy and money into collections that I can no longer keep. However, I am thankful for the joy each purchase brought me. I have learned of my negative ways and now I am on the road to healing.

Chapter 15

Home at Last

I live in a house that I own. I even have my own bedroom. This is where I belong. The lovely brick house with three bedrooms and two full bathrooms is surrounded by magnolia trees, live oaks and longleaf pines. There are geraniums, roses, azaleas, ginger flowers and gardenias all around the house. The fragrance of the ginger flowers makes me high with energy as I observe them each morning. My neighbors admire my ginger flowers because they stand out like kings ruling over my garden. I even have a linden tree, a plum tree, a fig tree, a kumquat tree and a lemon tree. My kumquat tree produces so many kumquats that I invite my friend Margaret to come over and pick some for the jam she makes. My kumquats are a beautiful orange, adding color to the green surrounding it. Nature finally surrounds me and can be seen from every window. The bright green surroundings and the quietness are a pleasant reprieve from the noise of foreign countries.

I disliked living in rented apartments and houses in Germany because the landlords felt they could come by at any time. I felt that I had no privacy in rented places, so I am grateful for my own house. In addition, the apartments that I rented in Stuttgart were sold, so I had to move to three different apartments during the ten years I lived there. Moving is costly and time-consuming. Every time I moved, I felt like

I was starting all over again. The moving did not help me feel like I belonged. I had to adjust to new neighbors, new smells in the building and new furniture arrangements in the apartment. Will my couch or lounging chair fit into the apartment? was always a question in my mind. During the second move, I had to discard my couch because it was too big and a new one had to be purchased.

The smell of sauerkraut is one that I could not tolerate, so if someone in the building made it, I would have to wear a mask to not smell it. In one apartment, I lived on the fifth floor and the elevator did not work for several days. I had to carry groceries up five flights of stairs. At the end, I thought I would collapse. I never want to live in an apartment building again. I had my fill of apartment living for my lifetime. Approaching Turkey Creek and stopping to watch the water flow in the creek energizes me, making me feel like I belong in the universe. Connecting with nature has become a better high than shopping. I discover a new tree or plant each day while I walk, so the desire to move to another place has diminished. I return home from my nature walk feeling like I can conquer the world.

I can write and reflect on my life and my daily experiences. I have stopped bringing things in and am now discarding things. I make weekly trips to Goodwill with clothes and shoes that I have not worn in a year. I gave away a beautiful pair of blue suede shoes that I never wore. They no longer need to remain in my closet. I am finally able to get rid of things. The memory of an uncluttered and clean apartment in California helps me to declutter in Niceville. I am proud to have friends come over and spend time with me. I am on the way to creating an uncluttered house. I will invite people over to share fellowship with them. We create our own loneliness by not reaching out to people who have the same interests as we do. I have learned to sit down, be still and pray about my impulses to move to a new place. A friend kindly said, "Stop the moving. This is where you belong. Your house reflects you."

Even when others ask why I remain in Niceville; I can honestly say, "I belong here." The physical desire to move stopped when another pair of eyes could see me in Niceville.

I developed a dry cough when I moved into my house in Niceville. All the medications that the doctors had given me did not work. One doctor said he was stumped and had no answers. As the cough continued for several months, I kept looking for other doctors. I finally visited a Foundational Medicine doctor, and she thought the clutter and perhaps mold were causing my cough. As I started to declutter different areas of the house, I noticed that the cough subsided. I cleaned out my bedroom. What a difference that made in my sleep! No coughing at night occurred. The doctor was right; my home was making me sick. That was a good lesson for me and helped to bring about change. I had to get sick to bring this change about. Now my medicine is walking, journaling, praying and keeping my home uncluttered. I have found a strong, self-care routine.

Niceville is quiet and peaceful. I can reflect and write without distraction from outside noises. Even when it is hot and humid outside, I can relax and be cool in my air-conditioned home. I can look out my window and admire my trees and flowers. I am grateful that in the evening of my life I have found a place where I belong. Life wasn't always this way for me. There were many journeys before I landed in Niceville, Florida. It took me a long time to realize that stuff and moving are not substitutes for my father and belonging. Writing my memoir helped me become aware of bad medicine. I no longer need to keep on buying things and moving.

I am settled and peaceful.

End

Epilogue

I left New York City on March 2, 2020 just before COVID-19 hit. I was fortunate I did not contract the virus, and I saw New York City as I remembered it with its many restaurants, Broadway shows and department stores. With the closure of many places, New York City is a different place. COVID-19 has changed people's lives. Places are closed, we wear masks and we practice social distancing.

For an introvert like me, staying home has enabled me to declutter my house and curtail going to estate and yard sales. I no longer bring in things, but instead I make regular trips to Goodwill. It has enabled me to get deeper into Jungian ideas. It has allowed me to take Zoom courses and interact with people instead of traveling to take courses to keep up my license. I have been able to write more this year, including this memoir. I had a website developed to enhance my practice of Jungian Analysis.

I do miss physical contact with people. I no longer shake hands with my clients or with my pastor after a sparsely populated church service. The longing for physical touch is one of the aspects I miss most. Physical touch is an important aspect of human communication, so once the virus is contained and we can greet one another with physical touch, our hunger might be satisfied.

04167962-00967712

Printed in the United States
by Baker & Taylor Publisher Services